Ultimate Price

Testimonies of Christians
Who Resisted the Third Reich

Ultimate Price

Testimonies of Christians
Who Resisted the Third Reich

✝

Selected with an Introduction by

ANNEMARIE S. KIDDER

ORBIS  BOOKS
Maryknoll, New York 10545

Copyright © 2012 by Annemarie S. Kidder

Published by Orbis Books, Box 302, Maryknoll, NY 10545-0302.

Library of Congress Cataloging-in-Publication

Ultimate price : testimonies of Christians who resisted the Third Reich / selected with an introduction by Annemarie S. Kidder.
 p. cm.
 ISBN 978-1-57075-955-0 (pbk.)
 1. Christian martyrs—Germany—Biography. 2. Germany—History—20th century. 3. Germany—Politics and government—1913-1945. 4. Anti-Nazi movement—Germany—Biography. I. Kidder, Annemarie S.

BR1608.5.U48 2012
940.53'18320922—dc23
[B]   2011044567

CONTENTS

INTRODUCTION

In ancient Greece, the birthplace of democracy, self-declared rulers who violated the rights of the people by maintaining power through weaponry were considered tyrants. When in 514 B.C., the tyrant Hipparch was murdered by Harmodios and Aristogiton, his murderers were subsequently celebrated by the people as freedom fighters and heroes.

In the history of nations, unjust power often led to two types of resistance: private resistance in the form of internal rejection, covert criticism, and passive resistance, such as hunger strikes or suicide; and active, organized resistance, ranging from the distribution of pamphlets to campaigning, speeches, sabotage, or coups and armed revolt.

During times of war, the term "resistance" is commonly associated with an organized, armed revolt. But in relation to the Nazi era, between 1933 and 1945, resistance has come to be viewed as any conscious attempt to stand up against the National Socialist regime. Despite the regime's tactics that sought to dominate the entire person by means of terror, torture, and spying, German society was not as centralized and self-enclosed as the regime had hoped. Despite enormous pressure, even by 1941 the majority of Germans were not members of the Nazi party or one of its organizations. Many stood aside, neither harboring the wish for a return to democracy nor preparing for resistance. Still, by 1939 about 300,000 people were in prison or camps due to political resistance activity. More than 5,000 active resisters had to pay with their lives, and another

15,000 were executed for such military crimes as desertion and subversive activity.

In these biographical sketches, we find people compelled by their Christian faith to oppose the political ideologies and measures of the Nazi regime. What is it that drove them to confront the authorities at the risk of their own lives? What convinced them, long before the verdict of history vindicated their dissenting opinions and actions, that defending the dignity of human life meant standing in solidarity with those bound to be imprisoned, tortured, killed?

Many others could have been included in this volume, but this small sample must suffice to show the diverse motivations that compelled Catholics and Protestants, clergy and laity to resist public opinion and to swim against a tidal wave of mass obeisance, gullibility, and fear.

What unites the people we meet here is a deep love for the church and a wide-awake Christian faith. Some held a church office, served on the theological faculty of a university, worked in the church media, or were active in Christian circles. Others were members or associates of a religious order such as the Society of Jesus or the Franciscans. Invariably they believed that Jesus Christ prompted them to act and speak, as he did, on behalf and in defense of those deprived of their voice and human rights. Certainly, these men and women were beset by ambiguities and internal wrestling. But they also pressed on to attend the echoes of conscience in their heart, to comprehend the meaning of justice and obedience and God's boundless love for all people. Their lives speak of a power that allows one to relinquish personal safety for safekeeping in God, to take risks and lose one's life in order to find it.

We cannot presume to fully understand these prophets and witnesses of an era marked as one of Western history's bleakest. What was it like for them to have their fellow parishioners, superiors, and family members challenge the troubling convictions they had reached and the consequences they were willing to bear? As we trace their spiritual writings we allow them to shepherd us into heeding our own conscience in times that beg for discernment among contending voices of authority. They bid us examine our loyalties to kin and country in light of Christ's claims. And they prod us unremittingly into siding with those Christ calls "the least of these," with whom he so identifies.

EARLY CHRISTIAN RESISTANCE

After Hitler's rise to power in January 1933, several political resistance groups sprang up. Chief among them were Communists, of whom more than 15,000 were arrested in the course of the year 1933 alone. Socialist-oriented democrats were perhaps the second-largest group of resisters, distributing pamphlets and painting political slogans on house walls. Anyone engaged in such activities or assisting in them was subject to imprisonment, torture, deportation to a concentration camp, or execution.

Nearly sixty active resistance groups[1] are known to have been operating during the Nazi era, their members at constant risk of being discovered, imprisoned, and executed—as, in fact, many of them were. This constant danger kept these groups relatively small, so that many if not most of them ranged in size from a handful to a few dozen members and confidants. Groups also collaborated with other groups, though such exchanges and mutual support increased the risk of being discovered, as did making and maintaining contacts with sympathizers and recruiting collaborators in Germany and abroad. Nonetheless, the groups' overall effect in their attempts to stem the tide of state control and to sway public opinion was modest. Germany's two state church bodies, Protestant and Catholic, were in a much better position to do so.

From the beginning, Hitler sought the centralization (*Gleichschaltung*) of all potential opponents, which included the churches, and their subordination to the Nazi domination of the political landscape. His aim was to destroy the influence of Christianity in Germany altogether. The structure and organization of the two large church bodies, Roman Catholic and Protestant, both essentially independent of state control,[2] demanded two distinct approaches. In June 1933, Hitler proposed centralizing the state's Protestant Church (*Evangelische Kirche*[3]), composed of twenty-eight regional churches (*Landeskirchen*), and putting it under the auspices of a new National Church structure and a Reich's bishop. The Reich's bishop was charged with promoting the Nazi agenda. Germany's Roman Catholic Church, on the other hand, derived its mandate directly from the pope in Rome, which meant that Hitler needed to enter into a direct alliance with the pope.

As early as July 1933, Hitler succeeded in the signing of a Concordat, a contract between the Holy See and the German nation. The treaty would endorse Hitler's leadership as Germany's head of state and grant him international recognition from the Vatican. Signed by Cardinal Eugenio Pacelli—later to become Pope Pius XII—and Franz von Papen, it granted Catholics the free and public practice of the Catholic religion and gave the Catholic Church freedom "to manage and regulate her own affairs independently" and to publish instructions, ordinances, and pastoral letters "without hindrance." It also ensured the state's "official protection" of members of the clergy in the exercise of their ecclesial functions and granted complete autonomy to religious orders and congregations. Moreover, the state guaranteed that Catholic religious instruction in

Germany's public schools would continue and that Catholic schools and the establishment of new ones would be ensured. In turn, German bishops, upon taking office, had to swear "an oath of fealty either to the Reich representative of the state concerned, or to the President of the Reich, according to the following formula: 'Before God and on the Holy Gospels I swear and promise, as becomes a bishop, loyalty to the German Reich and to the State of . . . . I swear and promise to honor the legally constituted government and to cause the clergy of my diocese to honor it. In the performance of my spiritual office and in my solicitude for the welfare and the interests of the German Reich, I will endeavor to avoid all detrimental acts which might endanger it.' "[4] Within two years, Hitler had violated all state guarantees anchored in the Concordat, while the bishops were expected to uphold their end of the contract.

By 1937 the anti-Catholic nature of Hitler's regime had become plain to Pope Pius XI. With the help of Michael Cardinal von Faulhaber (1869-1952) of Munich who drafted the document, the pope issued an encyclical on March 14, 1937, that priests were to read to their congregations throughout Germany on March 21, Palm Sunday. The forty-three-paragraph-long encyclical, titled "Mit brennender Sorge" ("With Burning Anxiety"), had to be smuggled into Germany and was secretly distributed among the Roman Catholic clergy. Sparking the immediate wrath of the Nazis, it took issue with the way National Socialism was persecuting Catholic clergy, women and men religious, and the Catholic laity by placing political ideology above Christian doctrine. The encyclical also sought to alert all Catholics in Germany to Hitler's false doctrine of a national God and a national religion. The encyclical opens with the following words: "It is with burning anxiety and growing surprise that We have long been following the painful trials of the Church and the increasing vexations which afflict those who have remained loyal in heart and action in the midst of a people that once received from St. Boniface the bright message and the Gospel of Christ and God's Kingdom."

In several points the encyclical explicitly criticizes Hitler's nationalist regime with its Aryan ideology, anti-Jewish hate propaganda, and blasphemous worship of Hitler as savior figure:

8. Whoever exalts race, or the people, or the State, or a particular form of State, or the depositories of power, or any other fundamental value of the human community—however necessary and honorable be their function in worldly things—whoever raises these notions above their standard value and divinizes them to an idolatrous level, distorts and perverts an order of the world planned and created by God; he is far from the true faith in God and from the concept of life which that faith upholds....

11. None but superficial minds could stumble into concepts of a national God, of a national religion; or attempt to lock within the frontiers of a single people, within the narrow limits of a single race, God, the Creator of the universe, King and Legislator of all nations before whose immensity they are "as a drop of a bucket" (*Isaiah* xl, 15).

12. The Bishops of the Church of Christ, "ordained in the things that appertain to God" (*Heb.* v, 1) must watch that pernicious errors of this sort, and consequent practices more pernicious still, shall not gain a footing among their flock. It is part of their sacred obligations to do whatever is in their power to enforce respect for, and obedience to, the commandments of God, as these are the necessary foundation of all private life and public morality; to see that the rights of His Divine Majesty, His name and His word be not profaned; to put a stop to the blasphemies, which, in words and pictures, are

multiplying like the sands of the desert; to encounter the obstinacy and provocations of those who deny, despise and hate God, by the never-failing reparatory prayers of the Faithful, hourly rising like incense to the All-Highest and staying His vengeance. . . .

16. Whoever wishes to see banished from church and school the Biblical history and the wise doctrines of the Old Testament, blasphemes the name of God, blasphemes the Almighty's plan of salvation, and makes limited and narrow human thought the judge of God's designs over the history of the world: he denies his faith in the true Christ, such as He appeared in the flesh, the Christ who took His human nature from a people that was to crucify Him; and he understands nothing of that universal tragedy of the Son of God who to His torturer's sacrilege opposed the divine and priestly sacrifice of His redeeming death, and made the new alliance the goal of the old alliance, its realization and its crown.[5]

Germany's Protestant church was being challenged by Hitler in a different way. It came with his creation of a *Reichskirche* (Reich's Church) and the appointment to Reich's bishop of Ludwig Müller in June 1933. Müller, a former army chaplain, enjoyed Hitler's confidence and the backing of a group of younger radical clergy, known as the Deutsche Christen ("German Christians"), or Nazi-Christians. The group claimed to be spearheading a national revival in Protestant churches. The Protestant church, they said, would partner with the state, "the swastika on our breasts, and the Cross in our hearts."[6] Following church elections that marked his overwhelming victory, Müller soon announced his intention, in step with the state's measures, to introduce into the church's structures the "Aryan paragraph," which would preclude Germans of Jewish descent from holding church offices and required those already in office to resign. This racial ideology sparked the dissent of Martin Niemöller (1892-1984), a leading Lutheran pastor in Berlin, who proceeded to organize the Pastors Emergency League (*Pastorennotbund*) in order to defend traditional Protestant doctrine. By the end of 1933, some 7,000 Protestant clergy members, or about one-third of the Protestant clergy in Germany, belonged to Niemöller's League. Unintentionally, the German Christians had driven clergy to join the league by calling into question the place of the Old Testament in Christian teaching and demanding a purging of all Jewish practices and vocabulary from the church's liturgies. However, the league proved ineffective in forming a united Protestant opposition to Hitler's tactics of dictatorship. For this reason, Lutheran Bishop Theophil Wurm (1868-1953) of Württemberg summoned a conference in April 1934 to lay the foundations for an alternative Protestant church structure, which would come to be known as the Confessing Church.

The Confessing Church, under the leadership of its Council of Brethren, was an association of Protestant pastors and lay people in Germany who opposed the German Christians in their alignment with Hitler's ideology. As such, the Confessing Church was an alternative federation of Germany's so-called Evangelical Church (*Evangelische Kirche*), the state's Protestant church. Of a total of twenty-eight regional churches, nineteen belonged to the Confessing Church. Composed of members of the regional churches (*Landeskirchen*) who were either Lutheran, Reformed, or United,[7] the Confessing Church drew largely on two different sections of Germany: the Protestant churches in the areas of Berlin and Prussia whose administrations had been fully appropriated (or, as a former Confessing Church pastor put it, completely "destroyed") by the Nazi regime and were highly motivated to create a new, separate

Confessing Church; and the Protestant churches in all other German areas that were "non-destroyed," hence more inclined, in the interest of self-preservation, to make compromises with the regime and the German Christians.[8] Approximately one quarter of Protestant pastors in the Evangelical Church of Germany belonged to the Confessing Church, while another quarter were Nazi-Christians, and the remaining 50 percent thought of themselves as "neutral." After a number of regional meetings of the Confessing Church, members of the council brought together representatives of Germany's various Protestant regional churches of Lutheran, Reformed, and United denominations at the Gemarke Church, Barmen, in the city of Wupperthal. At the meeting of May 29-31, 1934, 139 delegates attended; 53 of them were church members, six university professors, and the rest ordained ministers. The chief item of business was discussion of a theological declaration that would urge the Protestant churches in Germany to stand firm against an accommodation to National Socialism.

The result of this was the Barmen Declaration of May 1934, a theological statement that insisted on the Protestant church's right to control its own doctrinal affairs and government. The declaration was largely drafted by the Reformed theologian Karl Barth (1886-1968) of Bonn University. Earlier Barth had established himself as the originator of "dialectic theology," which called into question a culturally conditioned Protestant theology that stood in service of contemporary sociopolitical ideas. In Barth's estimate, the German Christians were enlisting and expanding upon this type of theology by seeking to validate the anti-Christian ideology of National Socialism. Barth insisted that the true church stood on the foundations of Reformation theology and rejected all totalitarian claims of the state. Referencing passages from the New Testament to substantiate each of its six points, the Barmen Declaration affirmed that members of the Confessing Church would remain loyal to the scriptures and to their true leader, Jesus Christ:

> In view of the errors of the 'German Christians' of the present Reich Church government which are devastating the church and are also thereby breaking up the unity of the German Evangelical Church, we confess the following evangelical truths:

1. "I am the way, and the truth, and the life: no one comes to the Father, but by me" (John 14:6). "Truly, truly, I say to you, he who does not enter the sheepfold by the door but climbs in by another way, that man is a thief and a robber. . . . I am the door; if anyone enters by me, he will be saved" (John 10:1, 9).

   Jesus Christ, as he is attested for us in Holy Scripture, is the one Word of God which we have to hear and which we have to trust and obey in life and in death.

   We reject the false doctrine, as though the church could and would have to acknowledge as a source of its proclamation, apart from and besides this one Word of God, still other events and powers, figures and truths, as God's revelation.

2. "Christ Jesus, whom God made our wisdom, our righteousness and sanctification and redemption" (I Cor. 1:30).

   As Jesus Christ is God's assurance of the forgiveness of all our sins, so in the same way and with the same seriousness is he also God's mighty claim upon our whole life. Through him befalls us a joyful deliverance from the godless fetters of this world for a free, grateful service to his creatures.

   We reject the false doctrine, as though there were areas of our life in which we would not belong to Jesus Christ, but to other lords—areas in which we would not need justification and sanctification through him.

3. "Rather, speaking the truth in love, we are to grow up in every way into him who is the head, into Christ, from whom the whole body [is] joined and knit together" (Eph. 4:15-16).

The Christian Church is the congregation of the brethren in which Jesus Christ acts presently as the Lord in Word and Sacrament through the Holy Spirit. As the church of pardoned sinners, it has to testify in the midst of a sinful world, with its faith as with its obedience, with its message as with its order, that it is solely his property, and that it lives and wants to live solely from his comfort and from his direction in the expectation of his appearance.

We reject the false doctrine, as though the church were permitted to abandon the form of its message and order to its own pleasure or to changes in ideological and political convictions.

4. "You know that the rulers of the Gentiles lord it over them, and their great men exercise authority over them. It shall not be so among you; but whoever would be great among you must be your servant" (Matt. 20:25, 26).

The various offices in the church do not establish a dominion of some over the others; on the contrary, they are for the exercise of the ministry entrusted to and enjoined upon the whole congregation.

We reject the false doctrine, as though the church, apart from this ministry, could and were permitted to give to itself, or allow to be given to it, special leaders vested with ruling powers."[9]

By 1935 Hitler realized that his plan of subordinating the Protestant church to party lines was not happening as planned.

The voice of the Confessing Church had led to warring factions within Protestant church politics, especially to a clash with the German Christians. In July 1935, Hitler established a new Ministry of Religious Affairs, charged with enforcing a centralized church government, and appointed as its new minister Hanns Kerrl. His ministry would seek to control all the external factors of the Protestant church's life in Germany and thus avert the unseemly disunity of earlier years. As it turned out, Kerrl's efforts were sabotaged from within and without: The more radical Nazi leaders were more inclined to root out Christianity altogether rather than seeking to bring the churches under Nazi influence; and the members of the Confessing Church continued to have reservations about the misuse of the state's power over the churches. When in 1941 Kerrl died, he was not replaced. By then, stamping out Christianity in Germany had become of secondary concern to Hitler: he had launched a war with the invasion of Poland in 1939, shifting energies and attention from internal to external domination.

LATER DEVELOPMENTS

The 1933 Concordat between the Vatican and the Hitler regime set the stage for the public stance of the Roman Catholic Church. The initial support the German bishops and the pope had given Hitler was hard to reverse. Only reluctantly did most bishops relinquish their illusions of the state's whole-hearted collaboration with the church. Similarly, the pope and his advisors continued to believe that the Nazi dictator could be brought to reason in his church policy. The Vatican's Cardinal Secretary of State, Eugenio Pacelli (1876-1958), who had been responsible for the signing of the Concordat and who in 1939 was elected pope as Pius XII, continued to object in private to the infringements of the Concordat and the regime's relentless attacks against the church, but publicly he declared his hopes for a negotiated settlement. The same policy, based on false judgment and miscalculations, was shared by other powers, including the leaders of European nations.

The failure of the Catholic hierarchy to confront Hitler left acts of resistance up to individual Catholics, including priests and bishops. Among members of the Catholic hierarchy in Germany who consistently opposed the regime's ideology and terror, special recognition belongs to Cardinal Michael von Faulhaber (1869-1952) of Munich, Bishop Konrad von Preysing (1880-1950) of Berlin, and Bishop Clemens August von Galen (1878-1946) of Münster. The vast majority of bishops and their fellow Catholics, however, tended to support the state in its expansionist foreign policy, rejection of democratic principles, and efforts to revitalize the nation's economy. Catholic protests arose largely in response to the state's secularizing measures in religious life and practice. Such measures included the dissolving of Catholic organizations and youth groups; pressure on parents to enroll their children in the Hitler Youth; the restriction or prohibition of pilgrimages, religious processions, and retreats; and the enforced substitution of the swastika for religious symbols such as the crucifix in schools. At one point, the outraged protests of hundreds of Catholic parents in defense of Catholic schools forced the Nazis to relent. Similar protests among Catholics took place in 1941 against the state's euthanasia campaign, which involved the systematic killing of adults and children with physical and mental disabilities, terminal illnesses, and birth defects. When the bishop of Münster, Clemens August von Galen, objected to these measures in his sermons, his protest effectively put a halt to the state's program of mass euthanasia.

Aware of the Catholic clergy's influence on their flock from the pulpit and through pastoral visits, the Nazi regime launched in 1935 a gigantic hate and slur campaign against Roman Catholic clergy as well as monks and nuns. With lurid headlines and fictitious reports, Nazi newspapers accused them of sexual crimes against children in their care, of sexual misconduct in monasteries and convents, and of infringing on currency laws by smuggling gold across German borders. A number of mock trials were also staged. The purpose of the campaign was to separate Catholics from their ecclesial leaders and weaken support of them and of the church in general. While the campaign's success was limited, in some cases even strengthening the solidarity between clergy and people, the majority of the German Catholic bishops continued to stress their loyalty to the state. Both the Catholic clergy and the Nazis could readily agree that Christianity and National Socialism, or Catholicism and National Socialism, were incompatible in the long run. But given the tepid response of Catholic leaders to national expansionism, the systematic campaign against Jews and other minorities, and the infringement of civil liberties, it was easy for the majority of the Catholic population to believe that one could be both a good Catholic and a good Nazi.

Among Protestants, sentiments toward the state were shaped by the biblical injunction of the Apostle Paul in Romans 13:1-2: "Let every person be subject to the governing authorities; for there is no authority except from God, and those authorities that exist have been instituted by God. Therefore whoever resists authority resists what God has appointed, and those who resist will incur judgment." As early as April 1933, Dietrich Bonhoeffer (1906-45) had urged Protestants to take a stand on the Nazis' ill treatment of Jews and the "Jewish question." In May 1936, the Confessing Church issued a statement sent to Hitler. In it, members objected to the imprisonment of pastors, the terror of the secret police, and the National Socialists' ideology of anti-Semitism: "If the Christian within the scope of the National Socialist worldview is forced to an anti-Semitism which requires hatred of Jews, the Christian commandment to love one's neighbor stands for him as a contrary law."[10] The following year, more than seven hundred pastors and associates of the Confessing Church were arrested and interrogated by the regime. But to Bonhoeffer the Confessing Church had not gone far enough in issuing a concrete stance of opposition, nor did its member churches sufficiently insist, as he did, that "outside the Confessing Church there is no salvation."[11]

Ambivalence reigned among Protestants as heirs to the Reformation and Luther's two-kingdom doctrine: where to draw the line between the kingdom of God and the kingdom of the world? The result of this ambivalence stifled any real growth of opposition and the effectiveness of the Confessing Church. Like their Catholic colleagues, Protestant clergy largely ignored or excused the Nazi excesses until it was too late. Their own nationalism and a traditional adherence to doctrines of authority, including biblical authority, precluded large-scale organizational efforts or protests. This miscalculation on the part of the Protestant churches, including the Confessing Church, was later acknowledged by one of the Confessing Church's leaders, Martin Niemöller. Arrested at the personal orders of Hitler in 1937, Niemöller would spend the next eight years in prisons and concentration camps. His internment sparked international protests and raised awareness abroad of the goals of the Confessing Church and the churches' struggle. Mahatma Gandhi, the leader of India's independence movement and advocate of nonviolent resistance, remarked: "I do not think that the suffering of Pastor Niemöller and of others have been in vain."[12]

In the course of his imprisonment, Niemöller's attitude in regard to the church's relationship to the state underwent a significant shift. Rather than standing in service to the country, the church, he thought, was responsible through the event of Christ's cross and resurrection to work for reconciliation among the nations, to address and overcome racial bigotry, and to help settle ideological divisions. After the war in numerous speeches he ruefully admitted that he had a share in the blame that allowed National Socialism to come to power and remain in it. In a well-known statement, he admitted, "When they arrested the Communists and Socialists, I said: I am not a Communist, so I did nothing. When they imprisoned the Jews, I said: I am not a Jew, so I did nothing. When they attacked the Catholics, I said: I am not a Catholic, so I did nothing. When they came for me, there was no one left."[13] After the war, an admission of guilt was formulated by a group of Protestant pastors, among them Niemöller and Bishop Wurm. The Stuttgart Declaration of Guilt was written on behalf of the entire German Protestant church by the Council of the Evangelical Church of Germany in October 1945: "We have fought for long years in the name of Jesus Christ against the spirit that found horrible expression in the National Socialist regime by force; but we charge ourselves for not having borne testimony with greater courage, prayed more consciously, and loved more ardently."[14] Eighteen pastors of the Confessing Church had been executed in concentration camps.

A smaller group of independent or "free" Protestant churches in Germany should be mentioned also. They were called "free" because congregations raised their own funds rather than enlisting a government agency to do their fundraising through the levying of taxes. Their membership comprising slightly less than 10 percent of the entire Christian population in Germany, the free churches were largely affiliated with such denominations as the Baptists, Methodists, Moravians, and Mennonites. Other independent or "free" religious associations were Germany's sects, such as the Mormons and the Jehovah's Witnesses. The free churches' somewhat separatist stance toward the state could have translated into firm resistance to the Nazi regime. Yet, according to Franklin H. Littell, "The free churches in Germany did not exploit their independence by producing a sturdy resistance. On the contrary, their leaders by and large collaborated,"[15] perhaps hoping that the newly formed Protestant Reich's Church would bring them a previously denied recognition. Among them, the Jehovah's Witnesses were the exception, suffering the highest percentage of martyrdom of any church during the Nazi era.

MUTUAL SUPPORT AND GUIDANCE FOR THE CONSCIENCE

Individual acts of resistance in Nazi Germany ranged from attempts to kill Hitler to the refusal to take the military oath or to committing suicide. Such resistance did not originate in a vacuum. The resister's conscience was honed by others of like mind as well as by reading biblical texts, confessional statements, pastoral letters, and papal encyclicals.

For Dietrich Bonhoeffer, three sources of collective support existed. They were the Confessing Church, the Kreisau Circle, and the opposition movement in the *Abwehr*. As a theologian and pastor he enjoyed the esteem and support of members of the Confessing Church, most notably by heading up the Confessing Church's seminary at Finkenwalde. Second, Bonhoeffer had been introduced to a group of intellectuals, among them members of the nobility, political officials, functionaries of labor unions, and Protestant and Catholic clergy. Together they were preparing a new form of government and church structure for Germany following the overthrow of Hitler's regime. Called the Kreisau Circle, a name the Nazis coined after apprehending several members in 1944, the group had been cofounded in 1940 by Helmuth James Count von Moltke (1907-45) and Peter Count Yorck von Wartenburg (1904-44), meeting on three occasions (in May and October of 1942, and in June 1943) on von Moltke's estate in Kreisau, with smaller gatherings in Berlin and Munich. About twenty men and women belonged to the group's nucleus, united in their opposition to National Socialism and their conviction that a new democratic Germany needed to be ordered along Christian principles such as civic and religious liberties and social justice. Bonhoeffer had met von Moltke in April 1942, four weeks before the first meeting of the Kreisau Circle, to which he had been most likely invited. With his colleague and friend Eberhard Bethge, Bonhoeffer later shared his positive impression of von Moltke, while adding that "we are not of the same opinion."[16] This diverging opinion also divided the Kreisau Circle and concerned the question whether to be content with ideological resistance or to forcefully eliminate Hitler and his key leaders. Along with some of the Kreisau Circle members, Bonhoeffer was convinced that one needed to put "a spoke in the wheel" of the regime of the "Anti-Christ" and eliminate Hitler, while von Moltke rejected the use of violence. Bonhoeffer was drawn to a third group of resisters whose members shared his convictions about tyrannicide, the opposition movement within the *Abwehr*, Hitler's military operation team, which had established contact with the Kreisau Circle. With the help of his brother-in-law, Hans von Dohnanyi (1902-45), Bonhoeffer had enlisted in the *Abwehr* after returning from a brief exile in the United States and quickly became implicated in the plot on Hitler's life.

In 1943, the Kreisau Circle had finalized its "Principles" to be put in effect when the time came for Germany's restructuring after Hitler's demise: "The government of the German

Reich considers Christianity the foundation for the moral and religious renewal of our nation to overcome both hatred and lies for the rebuilding of the European community of nations. . . . For this reason, the Reich's government is determined to realize by all means possible the following indispensable internal and external demands." Of the total of seven principles and demands for establishing a new government, the first three were as follows:

1. The crushed principles of law and justice have to be raised up again and become the governing structure of all human life. Under the tutelage of conscientious and independent judges, who do not fear human beings, they are the foundation for a future culture of peace.
2. Freedom of religion and the conscience is guaranteed. . . .
3. To break with the totalitarian control of the conscience and to recognize the inviolable dignity of the human person as the foundation of the newly devised structure of law and peace. Every person fully collaborates in the various social, political, and international areas of life. The right for work and property is protected by law without regard for race, nationality, and religious affiliation.[17]

As early as 1938, von Moltke had recruited members from his own circle of friends. Thus, the Kreisau Circle would come to include representatives of Germany's two major denominations, Protestant and Roman Catholic. Among them were the Protestant theologian Eugen Gerstenmaier (1906-86); the Protestant pastor Harald Poelchau (1903-72); and three Jesuit priests from Munich, Alfred Delp (1907-45), Lothar König (1906-46), and Augustin Rösch (1893-1963). The Jesuit provincial Rösch had recruited both Delp and König for work with the Kreisau Circle.

When von Moltke was arrested on January 19, 1944, several

Kreisau Circle members appealed to the opposition movement in the *Abwehr* that had gathered around Claus Count Schenk von Stauffenberg (1907-44). In August 1943, von Stauffenberg had joined a group of collaborators who had been trying to kill Hitler. The circle had as its key leader the Army General Ludwig Beck (1880-1944). After three failed attempts on Hitler's life, preparations began in the spring of 1944 for another attempt in the summer of that year. On July 20, 1944, at Hitler's headquarters "Wolfsschanze," von Stauffenberg placed a bomb hidden in a briefcase next to the chair where Hitler was going to sit a few minutes later. According to the "Plan Walküre," all the power centers of the National Socialists were to be shut down following Hitler's death, and the new government structure suggested by members of the Kreisau Circle was to take effect, so that peace talks could be conducted with the Allies. One of the members of the Kreisau Circle, Carl Goerdeler (1884-1945), was slated to become the new Reich's chancellor and the Army General Beck the Reich's president ("Reichsführer"). In contrast to the democratic Principles of the Kreisau Circle, the framework for a new government drafted by Goerdeler and Beck in 1944 gave preference to a future German monarchy.

Von Stauffenberg's attack on Hitler's life failed, killing several officers but not Hitler. On the very day of the attack, the Nazis were able to trace the conspirators back to the circle around von Stauffenberg and several members of the Kreisau Circle. Von Stauffenberg and several others were arrested and executed the same day. The subsequent chase for collaborators in the assassination attempt led to thousands of arrests. Two hundred people were executed on account of their direct connection with the attack or for their connections with von Stauffenberg; among them were Bonhoeffer, von Dohnanyi, and Delp.

The Jesuit Rupert Mayer (1876-1945) in Munich and the

Cathedral Provost Bernhard Lichtenberg (1875-1943) in Berlin found support and backing from their own bishops. From the start, both Bishop Faulhaber and Cardinal Preysing had been outspoken critics of the Nazis. Similarly, Sophie Scholl and her brother Hans found support among the other members of the White Rose in Munich and its branch in Hamburg. Collaboration among members of various groups lent momentum to the cause.

The case differed for those who engaged in acts of individual passive resistance. In their deliberations and decision making, Franz Jägerstätter (1907-43) and Jochen Klepper (1903-42) were largely guided by printed materials. Ambiguous about the goals of the Confessing Church, Jochen Klepper sought guidance in the writings of Martin Luther, the scriptures, Protestant hymnody, and newspaper articles about the Jewish response to the increasing persecution and deportation. In 1933, the regime had issued restrictive measures against Germany's half million Jews, sparking protests from the Jewish population; by 1938 such protests had been largely silenced by means of state violence, retaliation, and torture. Since 1941, and in the wake of systematic deportations to concentration camps, Jews were prohibited from emigrating, leaving them with two options: go into hiding or commit suicide. With the strident evacuations and deportations, more than 3,000 of the 164,000 remaining Jews opted for suicide, often joined in death by their non-Jewish spouses. For the Catholic layman Franz Jägerstätter, in struggling with his conscience, the sources of guidance and support were the bishop's pastoral letters, devotional materials, the scriptures, and the 1937 papal encyclical. It was by studying these documents and texts that his conscience compelled him to refuse the military oath.

Each person wrestled with a conscience held captive by God in the face of state violence, injustice, and lies. While their actions confess to the one who promised that in "dying we live," their writings testify to the internal struggle that perennially marks faithful discipleship. Both their actions and writings lend us courage to follow the one true leader, Jesus Christ, who vies for our attention and claims our loyalty today.

NOTES

[1]For a breakdown and descriptions of these groups, see Wolfgang Benz und Walter H. Pehle, eds., *Lexikon des deutschen Widerstandes* (Frankfurt: Fischer Verlag, 1994), 159-328.

[2]The two main churches in Germany, Roman Catholic and Protestant (or Evangelical), were autonomous from the state in governance and doctrinal issues. The taxes they levied on their members were collected by state revenue agencies for which the churches paid the agencies an administrative fee. Also, the two church bodies maintained a special status of protection of property under public law and freedom in doctrinal matters. The former church structure and governance in existence in Germany prior to Hitler's takeover was restored after World War II and is still in effect today.

[3]Often translated as Evangelical Church but rendered here as the state's Protestant Church.

[4]For the 1937 Concordat, see the Vatican's Web page, http://www.vatican.va.

[5]For the 1937 encyclical "Mit brennender Sorge" of Pope Pius XI, see Vatican Web site http://www.vatican.va.

[6]John S. Conway, *The Nazi Persecution of the Churches 1933-1945* (London: Weidenfeld and Nicolson, 1968), 45.

[7]Germany's Protestant Church, or Evangelical Church, was a loose federation of regional churches that were each autonomous. These regional churches, or *Landeskirchen*, were either Lutheran, Reformed, or United—the latter being a merger between "Lutheran" and "Reformed" groupings. Roughly speaking, a church's geographical proximity to either Saxony, the center of the Protestant Reformation under Martin Luther three centuries earlier, or to Switzerland, the center of Reformed thought, governed whether a regional church was in the Lutheran or Reformed tradition. This denominational landscape among Protestant regional churches still holds true today.

[8]Wolf-Dieter Zimmermann, "The Life of an Illegal Pastor: 1933-45," in *The Barmen Confession: Papers from the Seattle Assembly*, ed. Hubert G. Locke (Lewiston, NY: Edwin Mellen Press, 1986), 223-53.

[9]"The Theological Declaration of Barmen" in *The Constitution of the Presbyterian Church (U.S.A.): Part I: Book of Confessions* (Louisville, KY: Office of the General Assembly, 1999), 247-50; reprinted from Arthur C. Cochrane, *The Church's Confessions under Hitler* (Philadelphia: Westminster Press, 1962), 237-42.

[10]See Hans-Walter Krumwiede, *Geschichte des Christentums III. Neuzeit: 17. bis 20. Jahrhundert* (Stuttgart: Kohlhammer, 1977), 219.

[11]Zimmermann in *The Barmen Confession: Papers from the Seattle Assembly*, 233.

[12]Hans Joachim Oeffler et al., eds., *Martin Niemöller: Ein Lesebuch* (Köln: Pahl-Rugenstein Verlag, 1987), 85.

[13]During his 1947 speeches in the United States Niemöller frequently recited this poem.

[14]Stewart Winfield Herman, *The Rebirth of the German Church* (London: S.C.M. Press, 1946), 137.

[15]Franklin H. Littell, "The Church Struggle and Religious Liberty," in *The Barmen Confession: Papers from the Seattle Assembly*, 175-95, 179.

[16]Eberhard Bethge and Victoria Barnett, *Dietrich Bonhoeffer: A Biography* (Minneapolis: Fortress Press, 2000), 755.

[17]Walter Hofer, ed., *Der Nationalsozialismus: Dokumente 1933-1945* (Frankfurt: Fischer, 1983), 333ff; see the Web site of the Bundeszentrale für politische Bildung, "Widerstand traditioneller Eliten," http://www.bpb.de.

DIETRICH BONHOEFFER
(1906-45)

Preacher, Teacher, Spy

Weeks prior to the outbreak of World War II (1939-45), one of Germany's most promising theologians and pastors returned from the safe haven of America to his Nazi-haunted homeland. His friends tried to dissuade him. But he replied, "I will have no right to participate in the reconstruction of Christian life in Germany after the war if I do not share the tribulations of this time with my people." After his return, he enlisted in the military intelligence of the Nazi regime called the Abwehr, continued leadership in the Confessing Church—an alternative to Hitler's centralized state church, and joined a secret circle of leaders who were drafting a new German constitution and a postwar rebuilding plan. Convinced of the need to put a spoke in the wheel of an evil regime, he became involved with a circle that would attempt to kill Hitler. Imprisoned for eighteen months on relatively minor charges, his involvement in the failed conspiracy was eventually discovered. In April of 1945, Hitler himself ordered the execution by hanging of the thirty-nine-year-old Lutheran pastor. Today his name is included in most ecumenical dictionaries of Christian martyrs and saints and his name stands for active Christian resistance to the state's abuse of power and privilege.

Born in Breslau, Dietrich Bonhoeffer grew up in Berlin, Germany's capital and the seat of the Reichstag. His father was one of the leading physicians and neurologists of the time, and his mother was a teacher. The family was well off, with a staff of servants, and the mother home-schooled the six children. Bonhoeffer graduated two years early from high school, completed his doctoral studies in theology, and received a teaching post on the theological faculty at Berlin. Too young to be ordained into the pastorate, Bonhoeffer served as a curate to a German-speaking church in Barcelona, Spain. A scholarship took him to Union Theological Seminary in New York for the academic year 1930-31, where he was introduced to the social gospel, the two Niebuhr brothers, African American spirituals, and pacifism. Ordained a Lutheran pastor upon his return, Bonhoeffer taught at the University of Berlin from 1931 to 1933 on systematic theology, philosophy, the nature of the church, and Christology. He also held confirmation classes in a poor section of Berlin, coauthored a new catechism for his students, and founded a gathering place for unemployed youth and young adults. In 1932, Bonhoeffer bought a cottage near Berlin to make it a place where students could meet for religious discourse. From this circle emerged those who would become his allies in the resistance movement. His reputation spread, drawing considerable numbers of people to hear him preach.

Between 1933 and 1935, Bonhoeffer served as pastor of two German-speaking Protestant churches in London, made plans to visit India to study the nonviolent resistance methods of Gandhi, and upon his return founded a seminary for pastors who had joined a movement opposing the Nazi regime. The Confessing Church, a small yet influential resistance movement among German-speaking Protestant pastors, was founded by Martin Niemöeller and Karl Barth, among others, and Bonhoeffer played a key role in it. Upon the seminary's closing, Bonhoeffer wrote Life Together, published in 1938, a summary of life in the Christian community based on biblical insights and his personal experience of living in makeshift housing with some twenty-five student vicars. Shortly thereafter he wrote The Cost of Discipleship, which included a commentary on Jesus' Sermon on the Mount. Both books were "the distillation of his fundamental message—What it means to live with Christ." With the seminary's closing by the Nazis, Bonhoeffer was banned first from preaching, then teaching, and finally any kind of public speaking.

In June 1939, Bonhoeffer visited the United States again and was urged by his friends to stay. He refused, acting in accord with his view "that a Christian must accept his responsibility as a citizen of this world where God has placed him." Upon his return in July, he joined the military intelligence office of the Abwehr, where a small group was considering the overthrow of the National Socialist regime by killing Hitler. Between tasks on behalf of the Confessing Church and the resistance movement, Bonhoeffer wrote chapters for his book Ethics, which he hoped would be the summation of his life's work. Arrested on April 5, 1943, after money used to help Jews escape to Switzerland was traced to him, Bonhoeffer was imprisoned in Berlin, Tegel prison, for a year and a half. The prison guards allowed for a courier system to family and friends, thereby preserving many of his papers and letters. The collected prison writings were published posthumously by his friend Eberhard Bethge in 1950 and 1951, and in an expanded version in 1970, translated into English as Letters and Papers from Prison but titled in German "Resistance and Surrender" (Widerstand und Ergebung: Briefe und Aufzeichnungen aus der Haft). Within months of the unsuccessful plot on Hitler's life on July 20, 1944, Bonhoeffer's connections with the conspirators were discovered. From Tegel, he was moved to a series of prisons, ending up at Flossenbürg, where he was executed by hanging April 9, 1945, just three weeks before Hitler's suicide and the subsequent liberation of the city. Also hanged for their parts in the conspiracy were his brother Klaus and his brothers-in-law Hans von Dohnanyi and Rüdiger Schleicher.

Central to Bonhoeffer's thought is Jesus Christ as the sole savior of the world in whom God took on human form and by whose death was accomplished the reconciling of the world with God. Resulting from Christ's work is absolute freedom for the Christian, a freedom that prompts concrete action in the world, even putting "a spoke in the wheel" of the state to prevent evil and suffering. Departure from this center, whether in dialogue with other religions, ideologies, or daily life means renouncing Christianity. The radius and extension built around the center that is Christ is the church. It exists for the sake of the world, not for its own benefit, and its aim is to proclaim and work toward reconciliation between the world and God, which ultimately means working for peace. When the church and Christians fail to enact the kingdom principles that spring from a radical discipleship of Christ, a discipleship of "costly grace" even unto death, they need to beg the world and people for forgiveness for having failed and betrayed them.

* * *

In 1923, Bonhoeffer began his study of theology, completing the first two semesters at Tübingen and the rest at Berlin. After his first theological examination and his 1927 dissertation on the communion of saints, Sanctorum Communio, he served for a year as assistant pastor to a German-speaking Lutheran parish in Barcelona, Spain. While there, Bonhoeffer penned thoughts for the foundation of a Christian ethic that would enable Christians to shed the worn codes and "rusty swords" of a previous generation and make room for ethical guidelines by which to respond to contemporary problems. On January 25,

1929, Bonhoeffer presented to his congregation the sermon-lecture titled "What Is a Christian Ethic?"

For the Christian there are no ethical principles by means of which he could perhaps civilize himself. Rather must a direct relationship to God's will be ever sought afresh. I do not do something again today because it seemed to me to be good yesterday, but because the will of God points out this way to me today. That is the great moral renewal through Jesus, the renunciation of principles, of rulings, in the words of the Bible, of the Law, and this follows as a consequence of the Christian idea of God; for if there was a generally valid moral law, then there would be a way from man to God—I would have my principles, so I would believe myself assured *sub specie aeternitatis*. So, to some extent, I would have control over my relationship to God, so there would be a moral action without immediate relationship to God. And, most important of all, in that case I would once again become a slave to my principles. I would sacrifice man's most precious gift, *freedom*.

When Jesus places men immediately under God, new and afresh at each moment, he restores to mankind the immense gift which it had lost, freedom. Christian ethical action is action from freedom, action from the freedom of a man who has nothing of himself and everything of his God, who ever and again lets his action be confirmed and endorsed by eternity. The New Testament speaks of this freedom in great words. . . .

For the Christian there is no other law than the law of freedom, as the New Testament paradoxically puts it. No generally valid law which could be expounded to him by others, or by himself. The man who surrenders freedom surrenders his very nature as a Christian. The Christian stands free, without any protection, before God and before the world, and he alone is wholly responsible for what he does with the gift of freedom.

Now through this freedom the Christian becomes creative in ethical action. Acting in accordance with principles is unproductive, imitating the law, copying. Acting from freedom is creative. The Christian chooses the forms of his ethical action as it were from eternity, he puts them sovereign in the world, as his act, his creation from the freedom of a child of God. The Christian himself creates his standards of good and evil for himself. Only he can justify his own actions, just as only he can bear the responsibility. The Christian creates new tables, a new Decalogue, as Nietzsche said of the Superman. Nietzsche's Superman is not really, as he supposed, the opposite of the Christian; without knowing it, Nietzsche has here introduced many traits of the Christian made free, as Paul and Luther describe him. Time-honored morals—even if they are given out to be the consensus of Christian opinion—can never for the Christian become the standard of his actions. He acts, because the will of God seems to bid him to, without a glance to the others, at what is usually called morals, and no one but himself and God can know whether he has acted well or badly. In ethical decision we are brought into the deepest solitude, the solitude in which a man stands before the living God. No one can stand beside us there, no one can take anything from us, because God lays on us a burden which we alone must bear. Our "I" awakes only in the consciousness of being called, of being claimed by God, knowing myself to confront eternity alone. And because in the solitude I come face to face with God, I can only know for myself, completely personally, what is good and what is evil. There are no actions which are bad in themselves—even murder can be justified—there is only faithfulness to God's will or deviation from it; there is similarly no law in the sense of a law containing precepts, but only the law of freedom, i.e. of a man's bearing his responsibility alone before God and himself. But because the law remains superseded once for all and because it follows from the Christian idea of God that there can be no more law, the ethical commandments, the apparent laws of the New Testament must also be understood from this standpoint. . . .

Thus even in our time only one thing can be repeated, over and over again: in ethical decisions a man must put himself under the will of God, he must consider his action *sub specie aeternitatis* and then, however it turns out, it will turn out rightly. Now, day by day, hour by hour, we are confronted with unparalleled situations in which we must make a decision, and in which we make again and again the surprising and terrifying discovery that the will of God does not reveal itself before our eyes as clearly as we had hoped. This comes out because the will of God seems to be self-contradictory, because two ordinances of God seem to conflict with one another, so that we are not in a position to choose between good and evil, but only between one evil and another. . . .

But through this freedom from the law, from principle, the Christian must enter into the complexity of the world; he cannot make up his mind *a priori*, but only when he himself has become involved in the emergency and knows himself called by God. He remains earthbound, even when his desire is towards God; he must go through all the anxiety before the laws of the world; he must learn the paradox that the world offers us a choice, not between good and evil, but between one evil and another, and that nevertheless God leads him to himself even through evil. He must feel the gross contradiction between what he would like to do and what he must do; he must grow mature through this distress, grow mature through not leaving hold of God's hand, in the words "Thy will be done." A glimpse of eternity is revealed only through the depths of our earth, only through the storms of a human conscience. The profound old saga tells of the giant Antaeus, who was stronger than any man on earth; no one could overcome him until once in a fight someone lifted him from the ground; then the giant lost all the strength which had flowed into him through his contact with the earth. The man who would leave the earth, who would depart from the present distress, loses the power which still holds him by eternal, mysterious forces. The earth remains our mother, just as God remains our Father, and our mother will only lay in the Father's arms him who remains true to her. That is the Christian's song of earth and her distress.

All the examples which we have hitherto chosen have shown us that it is necessary for a man to be involved in the concrete situation and from there to direct his gaze towards eternity, contending afresh in the ambiguity of the situation always to decide in accordance with the will of God; the decision may then turn out as it will. And then ethics does not become once again a way from man to God, but remains like everything that men who know themselves to be freed from the world by Christ can do, a sacrifice, a demonstration of the weak will which springs from thankfulness for what God has done for us; a sacrifice, an offering, a demonstration which God can either accept or refuse; man's action springs from the recognition of the grace of God, towards mankind and towards himself, and man's action hopes for the grace of God which delivers him from the distress of the time.

—*No Rusty Swords*, pp. 43-48.

On January 30, 1933, Hitler had become the Reich's chancellor and immediately set out to align every aspect of German society with the principles of Nazism. These principles entailed absolute loyalty to his authority, a fierce hatred of communism and of the Jewish population, and the ideology that the German people were a superior race. On April 7 of that year, Hitler issued the Aryan Clauses, state-wide measures prohibiting Jews, or those married to Jews, from holding an office in the state or in the church. The measures affected government employees and pastors, among others. Bonhoeffer was one of the first to object with his 1933 theological essay titled "The Church and the Jewish Question." The essay is framed by Martin Luther quotes affirming Jewish Christians as full members of the church and the church's responsibility to reach out to the Jews with the message of Jesus Christ.

Without doubt, the Church of the Reformation has no right to address the state directly in its specifically political actions. It has neither to praise nor to censure the laws of the state, but must rather affirm the state to be God's order of preservation in a godless world; it has to recognize the state's ordinances, good or bad as they appear from a humanitarian point of view, and to understand that they are based on the sustaining will of God amidst the chaotic godlessness of the world. This view of the state's action on the part of the church is far removed from any form of moralism and is distinct from humanitarianism of any shade through the radical nature of the gulf between the standpoint of the Gospel and the standpoint of the Law. . . . The church cannot in the first place exert direct political action, for the church does not pretend to have any knowledge of the necessary course of history. Thus even today, in the Jewish question, it cannot address the state directly and demand of it some definite action of a different nature. But that does not mean that it lets political action slip by disinterestedly; it can and should, precisely because it does not moralize in individual instances, continually ask the state whether its action can be justified as legitimate action of the state, i.e. as action which leads to law and order, and not to lawlessness and disorder. It is called to put this question with great emphasis where the state appears to be threatened precisely in its nature as the state, i.e. in its function of creating law and order by means of force. It will have to put this question quite clearly today in the matter of the Jewish question. In so doing it does not encroach on the state's sphere of responsibility, but on the contrary fathers upon the state itself the whole weight of the responsibility for its own particular actions. . . .

All this means that there are three possible ways in which the church can act towards the state; in the first place, as has been said, it can ask the state whether its actions are legitimate and in accordance with its character as state, i.e. it can throw the state back on its responsibilities. Second, it can aid the victims of state action. The church has an unconditional obligation to the victims of any ordering of society, even if they do not belong to the Christian community. "Do good to all men." In both these courses of action, the church serves the free state in its free way, and at times when laws are changed the church may in no way withdraw itself from these two tasks. The third possibility is not just to bandage the victims under the wheel, but to put a spoke in the wheel itself. Such action would be direct political action, and is only possible and desirable when the church sees the state fail in its function of creating law and order, i.e. when it sees the state unrestrainedly bring about too much or too little law and order. In both these cases it must see the existence of the state, and with it its own existence, threatened. There would be too little law if any group of subjects were deprived of their rights, too much where the state intervened in the character of the church and its proclamation, e.g. in the forced exclusion of baptized Jews from our Christian congregations or in the prohibition of our mission to the Jews. Here the Christian church would find itself *in statu confessionis* and here the state would be in the act of negating itself. A state which includes within itself a terrorized church has lost its most faithful servant. But even this third action of the church, which on occasion leads to conflict with the existing state, is only the paradoxical expression of its ultimate recognition of the state; indeed, the church itself knows itself to be called here to protect the state *qua* state from itself and to preserve it. In the Jewish problem the first two possibilities will be the compelling demands of the hour. The necessity of direct political action by the church is, on the other hand, to be decided at any time by an "Evangelical Council" and cannot therefore ever be casuistically decided beforehand.

Now the measures of the state toward Judaism in addition stand in a quite special context for the church. The church of Christ has never lost sight of the thought that the "chosen people," who nailed the redeemer of the world to the cross, must bear the curse for its action through a long history of suffering. "Jews are the poorest people among all nations upon earth, they are tossed to and fro, they are scattered here and there in all lands, they have no certain place where they could remain safely and must always be afraid that they will be driven out . . ." (Luther, *Table Talk*). But the history of the suffering of this people, loved and punished by God, stands under the sign of the final home-coming of the people of Israel to its God. And this home-coming happens in the conversion of Israel to Christ. . . . The conversion of Israel, that is to be the end of the people's period of suffering. From here the Christian church sees the history of the people of Israel with trembling as God's own, free, fearful way with his people. It knows that no nation of the world can be finished with this mysterious people, because God is not yet finished with it. Each new attempt to "solve the Jewish problem" comes to nothing on the saving-historical significance of this people; nevertheless, such attempts must continually be made. This consciousness on the part of the church of the curse that bears down upon this people, raises it far above any cheap moralizing; instead, as it looks at the rejected people, it humbly recognizes itself as a church continually unfaithful to its Lord and looks full of hope to those of the people of Israel who have come home, to those who have come to believe in the one true God in Christ, and knows itself to be bound to them in brotherhood. Thus we have reached the second question.

The church cannot allow its actions toward its members to be prescribed by the state. The baptized Jew is a member of our church. Thus the Jewish problem is not the same for the church as it is for the state. From the point of view of the church of Christ, Judaism is never a racial concept but a religious one. What is meant is not the biologically questionable entity of the Jewish race, but "the people of Israel." . . .

What is at stake is by no means the question whether our German members of congregations can still tolerate church fellowship with the Jews. It is rather the task of Christian preaching to say: here is the church, where Jew and German stand together under the Word of God; here is the proof whether a church is still the church or not. No one who feels unable to tolerate church fellowship with Christians of Jewish race can be prevented from separating himself from this church fellowship. But it must then be made clear to him with the utmost seriousness that he is thus loosing himself from the place on which the church of Christ stands and that he is thus bringing to reality the Jewish-Christian idea of a religion based on law, i.e. is falling into modern Jewish Christianity.

—*No Rusty Swords*, pp. 222-29.

In a sermon preached at the Kaiser-Wilhelm Memorial Church in Berlin on May 28, 1933, titled "A Church of the World or a Church of the Word," Bonhoeffer contrasts the conflict be-tween a church obedient to the Word of God and a church beholden to idols. The sermon is rendered here in its entirety.

Priest against prophet, worldly church against the church of faith, the church of Aaron against the church of Moses—this is the eternal conflict in the church of Christ. And it is this conflict and its resolution that we are to consider today.

Moses and Aaron, the two brothers, of the same tribe, of the same blood, sharing the same history, going for part of the way side by side—then wrenched apart. Moses, the first prophet, Aaron, the first priest; Moses, called of God, chosen without regard of his person, the man who was slow of tongue, the servant of God, living solely to hear the Word of his Lord; Aaron, the man with the purple robe and the holy diadem, the consecrated and sanctified priest, who must maintain his service of God for the people. And now, in our story: Moses, called alone into the presence of the living God, high above on the mount of fear, between life and death in the thunder and lightning, to receive the law of the covenant of God with his people—and there down below in the valley, the people of Israel with their priest in his purple robe, sacrificing, far from God.

Why must Moses and Aaron be in conflict? Why cannot they stand side by side in the same service? Why must the church of Moses and the church of Aaron, the church of the Word and the worldly church turn time and again to different ways? The answer to this question is given in our text.

Moses is called up the mountain by God for his people. It is God's will to speak with him up there. The children of Israel know that. They know that up there Moses is standing, fighting, praying, suffering for them. He wears no purple robe, he is no priest; he is nothing at all, nothing but the servant who waits on the Word of his Lord, who is tormented when he is not given to hear this word. He is nothing—nothing but the prophet of his God. But the church of Aaron, the worldly church, cannot wait. It is impatient. Where has Moses got to? Why does he not come back? Perhaps we will not see him again. Where is he, with his God? "As for this Moses. . . we do not know what has become of him." It may be that he no longer exists, that he is dead.

These are the questions which the church of Aaron at all times puts to the church of the Word. "We cannot see it. Where are its works? What is its contribution? No doubt at all, it is dead." Do we not then understand that perhaps God himself is keeping Moses up on the mountain, that he is not yet letting him go because he still has something to say to him? Do we not understand that perhaps even today he is not yet letting the church of Moses go, the church whose wish is to hear only the Word of God, because he has still something to say in the quietness? Even God needs time with his prophets and with his church. Is it for us to be impatient? Certainly, the church of the Word is once again on Sinai, and in fear and trembling, amidst the thunder and lightning, stands up to the Word of God, waits, believes, prays, fights . . . For whom? For the church of Aaron, for the church down there in the valley, for the worldly church. The unwillingness of the worldly church to wait, its impatience, is the first stage of its clash with the church of the Word. So it has always been, and so it will continue to be.

"As for this Moses . . . we do not know what has become of him. Up, Aaron, make us gods, who shall go before us." That is the second stage, which follows immediately upon the first. The worldly church, the church of the priests, wants to see something. Now it will wait no longer. It must go to work for itself, see by itself, do by itself what God and the prophet are not doing. What is the use of the priest, what is the use of the church, if they are constantly kept on the watch? No, our church ought to have something. We want to see something in our church. We will not wait. You priests, you are sanctified, you are consecrated. You owe us something. Up, Aaron the priest, do your duty, attend to the divine service. God has left us, but we need gods. We need religions. If you cannot prevail with the Living God, make us gods yourself!

The concern expressed here is really not as bad as all that.

It is even a pious concern. "Away with gods!," but, "We need gods, religions, make us some!" They really want to keep a church with gods and priests and religion, but a church of Aaron—without God. And Aaron yields. He looks to his office, to his consecration; he looks to the people. He understands their impatience, their urge to do something, and their pious tumult only too well—and he yields. Come, you who have been abandoned by your God and by your prophet, make yourselves a god who will not leave you again, more splendid, more glorious than the God who has left us. Bring precious adornment, gold, jewelry, bring it as an offering. And they all come, without exception. They bring their precious offering to their own image of their god. They tear the ornaments from their bodies and throw them into the glowing mass from which Aaron now shapes the glittering, monstrous, golden calf. We hear it said that the people are not so ready for sacrifice. But those who talk like this do not know the world. The human race is ready for any sacrifice in which it may celebrate itself and worship its own work. The worldly church, the church of Aaron, is ready for any sacrifice if it is to be allowed to make its own God. The human race and the worldly church fall on their knees joyfully, and with smiles, before the god whom we make as it pleases us. But God finds little readiness with sacrifice. No, the church of Aaron does not stint, it is not mean, it is lavish with its god. Everything that is precious and valuable and holy to it is cast into the glow of the image of its god. Everything must contribute to the glorification of the god, so each one, according to his inclinations and his capabilities, throws his own ideals into the melting pot—and the orgy begins. The worldly church celebrates its triumph, the priest has shown his power, and how he himself stands in the middle in his purple robe and his holy diadem and worships the creation of his own hand. And round him the people prostrate themselves in ecstasy and look up at the god whom they have made in their own strength, at their own sacrifice. Who would want to stand aside from this pious joy, this unparalleled exuberance, this achievement of human will and ability? The worldly church now has its god, come, celebrate him, enjoy yourselves, play, eat, drink, dance, make merry, take yourselves out of yourselves! You have a god again. These are your gods, O Israel, who brought you up out of the land of Egypt! Come, behold, worship!

But there are rumblings on Sinai. For God shows Moses his faithless people. And Moses trembles for his people and comes hastily down from the mountain. He already hears the merry-making and the shouts of the dance and the tumult and the orgy. He already sees his brother in purple robe and holy diadem, and in the midst the golden god of the worldly church, the worldly god, the god of the priests, the god who is no God. There he stands amongst them, the unexpected prophet, high in his hands he swings the tables of the law, and they all must see it, the writing engraved by the hand of God. "I am the Lord your God, you shall have no other gods before me!" Dumb terror, dismay, seizes the worldly church at the sight. The party is over. The living God has come amongst them, he rages against them. What will happen? There—a sight unequalled, a fearful moment—and the tables of the law lie shattered on the idol, and the idol itself is broken in pieces and consumed. That is the end of the worldly church. God has appointed it. God has remained Lord. Lord, have mercy. . . !

Church of the priests against church of the Word, church of Aaron against church of Moses—this historical clash at the foot of Sinai, the end of the worldly church and the appearance of the Word of God, repeats itself in our church, day by day, Sunday by Sunday. Time and again we come together for worship in a worldly church, as a church which will not wait, which will not live from the invisible; as a church which makes its own gods; as a church which wants to have the sort of god which pleases it and will not ask how it pleases God; as a church which wants to do by itself what God will not do; as a church which is ready for any sacrifice in the cause of idolatry, in the cause of the divinization of human thoughts and values; as a church which appropriates to itself divine power in the priesthood. And we should go away again as a church whose idol lies shattered and destroyed on the ground, as a church which must hear afresh, "I am the Lord your God. . . ," as a church which is humbled as it is faced with this Word, as the church of Moses, the church of the Word. The impatient church becomes the quietly waiting church, the church anxious to see sights becomes the church of sober faith, the church which makes its own gods becomes the church which worships the One God. Will this church too find such devotion, such sacrifice?

But the rupture is not the end. Once again Moses climbs the mountain, this time to pray for his people. He offers up himself, "Reject me with my people, for we are still one. Lord, I love my brother." But God's answer remains dark, fearful, threatening. Moses could not make expiation. Who makes expiation here? It is none other than he who is priest and prophet in one, the man with the purple robe and the crown of thorns, the crucified Son of the Father, who stands before God to make intercession for us. Here, in his cross, there is an end of all idolatry. Here, the whole human race, the whole church, is judged and forgiven. Here God is wholly the God who will have no other god before him, but now also wholly God in that he forgives without limit. As the church which is always at the same time the church of Moses and the church of Aaron, we point to this cross and say, "This is your God, O Israel, who brought you out of slavery and will lead you evermore. Come, believe, worship!" Amen.

—*No Rusty Swords*, pp. 243-48.

In The Cost of Discipleship, *published in 1937, Bonhoeffer tries to formulate what it means to be a Christian and the true church. In doing so, he levels with the church in Germany, including its leaders, pastors, and members, as well as the so-called German Christians, who by their laxity, ignorance, or cowardice had distorted the Christian faith, thus enabling the apostasy that had come to replace obedience to Christ with blind loyalty to Hitler and the Nazi regime.*

Like ravens we have gathered around the carcass of cheap grace. From it we imbibed the poison which has killed the following of Jesus among us. The doctrine of pure grace experienced an unprecedented deification. The pure doctrine of grace became its own God, grace itself. Luther's teachings are quoted everywhere, but twisted from their truth into self-delusion. They say if only our church is in possession of a doctrine of justification, then it is surely a justified church! They say Luther's true legacy should be recognizable in making grace as cheap as possible. Being Lutheran should mean that discipleship is left to the legalists, the Reformed, or the enthusiasts, all for the sake of grace. They say that the world is justified and Christians in discipleship are made out to be heretics. A people became Christian, became Lutheran, but at the cost of discipleship, at an all-too-cheap price. Cheap grace had won.

But do we also know that this cheap grace has been utterly unmerciful against us? Is the price that we are paying today with the collapse of the organized churches anything else but an inevitable consequence of grace acquired too cheaply? We gave away preaching and sacraments cheaply; we performed baptisms and confirmations; we absolved an entire people, unquestioned and unconditionally; out of human love we handed over what was holy to the scornful and unbelievers. We poured out rivers of grace without end, but the call to rigorously follow

Christ was seldom heard. What happened to the insights of the ancient church, which in the baptismal teaching watched so carefully over the boundary between the church and the world, over costly grace? What happened to Luther's warnings against a proclamation of the gospel which made people secure in their godless lives? When was the world ever Christianized more dreadfully and wickedly than here? What do the three thousand Saxons whose bodies Charlemagne killed compare with the millions of souls being killed today? The biblical wisdom that the sins of the fathers are visited on the children unto the third and fourth generation has become true in us. Cheap grace was very unmerciful to our Protestant church.

Cheap grace surely has also been unmerciful with most of us personally. It did not open the way to Christ for us, but rather closed it. It did not call us into discipleship, but hardened us in disobedience. Moreover, was it not unmerciful and cruel when we were accosted by the message of cheap grace just where we had once heard the call to follow Jesus as Christ's call of grace, where we perhaps had once dared to take the first steps of discipleship in the discipline of obedience to the commandments? Could we hear this message in any other way than that it tried to block our way with the call to a highly worldly sobriety which suffocated our joy in discipleship by pointing out that it was all merely the path we chose ourselves, that it was an exertion of strength, effort, and discipline which was unnecessary, even very dangerous? The glowing wick was mercilessly extinguished. It was unmerciful to speak to such people since they, confused by such a cheap offer, were forced to leave the path to which Christ called them clutching instead at cheap grace. Cheap grace would permanently prevent them from recognizing costly grace. It could not happen any other way but that possessing cheap grace would mislead weaklings to suddenly feel strong, yet in reality, they had lost their power for obedience and discipleship. The word of cheap grace has ruined more Christians than any commandment about works.

In everything that follows, we want to speak up on behalf of those who are tempted to despair, for whom the word of grace has become frightfully empty. For integrity's sake someone has to speak up for those among us who confess that cheap grace has made them give up following Christ, and that ceasing to follow Christ has made them lose the knowledge of costly grace. Because we cannot deny that we no longer stand in true discipleship to Christ, while being members of a true-believing church with a pure doctrine of grace, but no longer members of a church which follows Christ, we therefore simply have to try to understand grace and discipleship again in correct relationship to each other. We can no longer avoid this. Our church's predicament is proving more and more clearly to be a question of how we are to live as Christians today.

—*Discipleship*, pp. 53-55.

(*On Matthew 7:15-20*) Jesus tells us that people cannot live for long under the cover of appearances. The time to bear fruit will come, the time of open difference will come. Sooner or later, their situation will be revealed. Whether the tree intends not to bear fruit does not matter at all. Thus the decisive moment of distinguishing one tree from another, fruit-bearing time, will reveal everything. Whenever times of decision come, revealing the difference between the world and the church-community, and they can come any day, in quite small, mundane decisions, as well as in the big ones, then it will be revealed what is bad and what is good. Then only reality persists, not appearances.

Jesus expects from his disciples that at such moments they will distinguish clearly between appearances and reality, and see the difference between ourselves and people who only appear to be Christian. That relieves them of all curious scrutinizing of other people, but it demands truthfulness and determination to recognize the decision God is making. It can happen at any moment that pseudo-Christians are torn out of our midst, or that we ourselves are revealed as pseudo-Christians. The disciples are called, therefore, to deeper communion [Gemeinschaft] with Jesus and to follow him more faithfully. The bad tree will be cut down and thrown into the fire. All its grandeur will not save it.

Verse 21. The separation caused by Jesus' call to discipleship goes even deeper. After the separation between world and community, between pseudo-Christians and true Christians, the next sorting out takes place within the confessing community of disciples. Paul says that no one can call Jesus Lord, except by the Holy Spirit (1 Cor. 12:3). No one can commit their life to Jesus and call him Lord out of their own reason, strength, and decision. But the possibility is considered here that someone could call Jesus Lord without the Holy Spirit, that is, without having heard Jesus' call. . . . The confession alone grants no claim on Jesus. On that day no persons can justify themselves on the basis of their confession. Being members of the church of the true confession is nothing we can claim before God. Our confession will not save us. If we think it will, then we commit Israel's sin of making the grace of our calling into a right before God. This is sin against the grace of the one who calls us. God will not ask us someday whether our confession was evangelical, but whether we did God's will. God will ask that of everyone, including us. . . . Those who do the will of God are called and forgiven by grace; they obey and follow. They do not understand their call to be a right, but to be judgment and pardon, and the will of God which alone they intend to obey. The grace of Jesus calls the doers: their deeds become genuine humility, genuine faith, genuine confession of the grace of the One who calls.

Verse 22. Confessors and doers are separated from each

other. Now the separation is driven in as far as it can go. Here, finally, those speak up who have survived the test up to now. They belong to the doers, but now they make demands based upon their deeds instead of upon their confession. . . . Jesus reveals to his disciples here the possibility of a demonic faith, which claims allegiance to him and which does wonderful deeds, to the point that they are indistinguishable from the deeds of true disciples of Jesus. They do works of love, miracles, perhaps even sanctify themselves, and yet deny Jesus and discipleship. It is just as Paul says in chapter 13 of the First Letter to the Corinthians about the possibility of preaching, prophesying, having all knowledge, even all faith to remove mountains—but without love, that is, without Christ, without the Holy Spirit. Yes, even more than this: Paul must even consider the possibility that the works of Christian love themselves, giving away one's goods, even so far as martyrdom, can be done—without love, without Christ, without the Holy Spirit. Without love—that means that in all those actions the deed of discipleship does not take place, that deed, whose doer is finally none other than the one who calls us, Jesus Christ himself. That is the deepest, the ultimate separation, which, of course, does not take place until the last judgment. But it will be a final one. —*Discipleship*, pp. 177-80.

The commentary on The Sermon on the Mount, which constitutes Part II of Bonhoeffer's Cost of Discipleship, *closes with a call to action.*

From a human point of view there are countless possibilities of understanding and interpreting the Sermon on the Mount. Jesus knows only one possibility: simply go and obey. Do not interpret or apply, but do it and obey. That is the only way Jesus' word is really heard. But again, doing something is not to be understood as an ideal possibility; instead, we are simply to begin acting.

This word, which I accept as valid for myself; this word, which arises from "I have known you," which immediately draws me into acting, into obedience, is the rock on which I can build a house. This word of Jesus coming from eternity can only be answered by simply doing it. Jesus has spoken; the word is his; our part is to obey. The word of Jesus keeps its honor, its strength, and power among us only by our acting on it. Then a storm can sweep over the house, but it cannot tear apart the unity with Jesus created by his word.

—*Discipleship*, pp. 181-82.

Since late 1940, Bonhoeffer had been hard at work at the Benedictine Ettal monastery in Bavaria on what he considered his major work, Ethics; *it was still in fragments at the time of his arrest in early April of 1943, and he continued working on it throughout his imprisonment without ever being able to finish it. Edited by his friend Eberhard Bethge, the manuscript was published posthumously in 1949. According to Bethge, Bonhoeffer wrote the portion titled "The Confession of Guilt" of the church in September or October of 1940, "at a time when Hitler had achieved his most astounding victory." This portion is an indictment of the church's failure to be a witness to Christ in the world and a call to repentance for having failed the world.*

[I]nnumerable individuals are united in the collective personality of the Church. It is in them and through them that the Church confesses and acknowledges her guilt.

The Church confesses that she has not proclaimed often and clearly enough her message of the one God who has revealed Himself for all times in Jesus Christ and who suffers no other gods beside Himself. She confesses her timidity, her evasiveness, her dangerous concessions. She has often been untrue to her office of guardianship and to her office of comfort. And through this she has often denied to the outcast and to the despised the compassion which she owes them. She was silent when she should have cried out because the blood of the innocent was crying aloud to heaven. She has failed to speak the right word in the right way and at the right time. She has not resisted to the uttermost the apostasy of faith, and she has brought upon herself the guilt of the godlessness of the masses.

The Church confesses that she has taken in vain the name of Jesus Christ, for she has been ashamed of this name before the world and she has not striven forcefully enough against the misuse of this name for an evil purpose. She has stood by while violence and wrong were being committed under cover of his name. And indeed she has left uncontradicted, and has thereby abetted, even open mockery of the most holy name. She knows that God will not leave unpunished one who takes His name in vain as she does.

The Church confesses herself guilty of the loss of the Sabbath day, of the withering away of her public worship, and of the contemptuous neglect of Sunday as a day of rest. She has incurred the guilt of restlessness and disquiet, and also of the exploitation of labor even beyond the working weekday, because her preaching of Jesus Christ has been feeble and her public worship has been lifeless. . . .

The Church confesses that she has witnessed in silence the spoliation and exploitation of the poor and the enrichment and corruption of the strong.

The Church confesses herself guilty towards the countless victims of calumny, denunciation and defamation. She has not convicted the slanderer of his wrongdoing, and she has thereby abandoned the slandered to his fate.

The Church confesses that she has desired security, peace and quiet, possessions and honor, to which she had no right, and that in this way she has not bridled the desires of men but has stimulated them still further.

The Church confesses herself guilty of breaking all ten commandments, and in this she confesses her defection from Christ. She has not borne witness to the truth of God in such a manner that all pursuit of truth, all science, can perceive that it has its origin in this truth. She has not proclaimed the justice of God in such a manner that all true justice must see in it the origin of its own essential nature. She has not succeeded in making the providence of God a matter of such certain belief that all human economy must regard it as the source from which it receives its task. By her own silence she has rendered herself guilty of the decline in responsible action, in bravery in the defense of a cause, and in willingness to suffer for what is known to be right. She bears the guilt of the defection of the governing authority from Christ. . . .

The justification of the western world, which has fallen away from Christ, lies solely in the divine justification of the Church, which leads her to the full confession of guilt and to the form of the cross. The renewal of the western world lies solely in the renewal of the Church, which leads her to the fellowship of the risen and living Jesus Christ.   —*Ethics*, pp. 113-17.

In 1942, Bonhoeffer recorded thematic reflections on the terror of the past ten years in which Germany had been under Nazi control. Titled "After Ten Years: A Reckoning made at New Year 1943," the manuscript was given by Bonhoeffer to his brother-in-law Hans von Dohnanyi and friends Hans Oster and Eberhard Bethge; another copy was hidden under the roof beams of his parents' house in Berlin, Charlottenburg.

WHO STANDS FAST?

The great masquerade of evil has played havoc with all our ethical concepts. For evil to appear disguised as light, charity, historical necessity, or social justice is quite bewildering to anyone brought up on our traditional ethical concepts, while for the Christian who bases his life on the Bible it merely confirms the fundamental wickedness of evil.

The "reasonable" people's failure is obvious. With the best intentions and a naïve lack of realism, they think that with a little reason they can bend back into position the framework that has got out of joint. In their lack of vision they want to do justice to all sides, and so the conflicting forces wear them down with nothing achieved. Disappointed by the world's unreasonableness, they see themselves condemned to ineffectiveness; they step aside in resignation or collapse before the stronger party. . . .

Who stands fast? Only the man whose final standard is not his reason, his principles, his conscience, his freedom, or his virtue, but who is ready to sacrifice all this when he is called to obedient and responsible action in faith and in exclusive allegiance to God—the responsible man, who tries to make his whole life an answer to the question and call of God. Where are these responsible people?

OF FOLLY

Folly is a more dangerous enemy to the good than evil. One can protest against evil; it can be unmasked and, if need be, prevented by force. Evil always carries the seeds of its own destruction, as it makes people, at the least, uncomfortable. Against folly we have no defense. Neither protests nor force can touch it; reasoning is no use; facts that contradict personal prejudices can simply be disbelieved—indeed, the fool can counter by criticizing them, and if they are undeniable, they can just be pushed aside as trivial exceptions. So the fool, as distinct from the scoundrel, is completely self-satisfied; in fact, he can easily become dangerous, as it does not take much to make him aggressive. A fool must therefore be treated more cautiously than a scoundrel; we shall never again try to convince a fool by reason, for it is both useless and dangerous.

If we are to deal adequately with folly, we must try to understand its nature. This much is certain, that it is a moral rather than an intellectual defect. There are people who are mentally agile but foolish, and people who are mentally slow but very far from foolish—a discovery that we make to our surprise as a result of particular situations. . . . We notice further that this defect is less common in the unsociable and solitary than in individuals or groups that are inclined or condemned to sociability. . . . The fact that the fool is often stubborn must not mislead us into thinking that he is independent. One feels in fact, when talking to him, that one is dealing, not with the man himself, but with slogans, catchwords, and the like, which have taken hold of him. He is under a spell, he is blinded, his very nature is being misused and exploited. Having thus become a passive instrument, the fool will be capable of any evil and at the same time incapable of seeing that it is evil. Here lies the danger of a diabolical exploitation that can do irreparable damage to human beings.

But at this point it is quite clear, too, that folly can be overcome, not by instruction, but only by an act of liberation; and so we have come to terms with the fact that in the great majority of cases inward liberation must be preceded by outward liberation, and that until that has taken place, we may as well abandon all attempts to convince the fool.

A FEW ARTICLES OF FAITH ON THE SOVEREIGNTY
OF GOD IN HISTORY

I believe that God can and will bring good out of evil, even out of the greatest evil. For that purpose he needs men who make the best use of everything. I believe that God will give us all the strength we need to help us to resist in all time of distress. But he never gives it in advance, lest we should rely on ourselves and not on him alone. A faith such as this should allay all our fears for the future. I believe that even our mistakes and shortcomings are turned to good account, and that it is no harder for God to deal with them than with our supposedly good deeds. I believe that God is no timeless fate, but that he waits for and answers sincere prayers and responsible actions.

SYMPATHY

. . . Christ kept himself from suffering till his hour had come, but when it did come he met it as a free man, seized it, and mastered it. Christ, so the scriptures tell us, bore the sufferings of all humanity in his own body as if they were his own—a thought beyond our comprehension—accepting them of his own free will. We are certainly not Christ; we are not called on to redeem the world by our own deeds and sufferings, and we need not try to assume such an impossible burden. We are not lords, but instruments in the hand of the Lord of history; and we can share in other people's sufferings only to a very limited degree. We are not Christ, but if we want to be Christians, we must have some share in Christ's large-heartedness by acting with responsibility and in freedom when the hour of danger comes, and by showing a real sympathy that springs, not from fear, but from the liberating and redeeming love of

Christ for all who suffer. The Christian is called to sympathy and action, not in the first place by his own sufferings, but by the sufferings of his brethren, for whose sake Christ suffered.

INSECURITY AND DEATH

. . . We still love life, but I do not think that death can take us by surprise now. After what we have been through during the war, we hardly dare admit that we should like death to come to us, not accidentally and suddenly through some trivial cause, but in the fullness of life and with everything at stake. It is we ourselves, and not outward circumstances, who make death what it can be, a death freely and voluntarily accepted.
—*Letters and Papers from Prison*, pp. 4-16.

From a letter to Eberhard Bethge written from the Tegel prison on July 21, 1944, the day after the unsuccessful attempt on Hitler's life by Claus von Stauffenberg.

During the last year or so I've come to know and understand more and more the profound this-worldliness of Christianity. The Christian is not a *homo religiosus*, but simply a man, as Jesus was a man—in contrast, shall we say, to John the Baptist. I don't mean the shallow and banal this-worldliness of the enlightened, the busy, the comfortable, or the lascivious, but the profound this-worldliness, characterized by discipline and the constant knowledge of death and resurrection. I think Luther lived a this-worldly life in this sense.

I remember a conversation that I had in America thirteen years ago with a French pastor. We were asking ourselves quite simply what we wanted to do with our lives. He said he would like to become a saint (and I think it's quite likely that he did become one). At the time I was very impressed, but I disagreed with him, and said, in effect, that I should like to learn to have faith. For a long time I didn't realize the depth of the contrast. . . .

I discovered later, and I'm still discovering right up to this moment, that it is only by living completely in this world that one learns to have faith. One must completely abandon any attempt to make something of oneself, whether it be a saint, or a converted sinner, or a churchman (a so-called priestly type!), a righteous man or an unrighteous one, a sick man or a healthy one. By this-worldliness I mean living unreservedly in life's duties, problems, successes and failures, experiences and perplexities. In so doing we throw ourselves completely into the arms of God, taking seriously, not our own sufferings, but those of God in the world—watching with Christ in Gethsemane. That, I think, is faith; that is *metanoia*; and that is how one becomes a man and a Christian (cf. Jer. 45!). How can success make us arrogant, or failure lead us astray, when we share in God's sufferings through a life of this kind?

—*Letters and Papers from Prison*, pp. 369-70.

SOURCES

Bohoeffer, Dietrich. 1965. *Ethics*. Ed. Eberhard Bethge. New York: Macmillan.

———. 1965. *No Rusty Swords: Letters, Lectures, and Notes 1928-1935 from the Collected Works*. New York: Harper and Row.

———. 1997. *Letters and Papers from Prison*. Ed. Eberhard Bethge. New York: Simon and Schuster.

———. 2003. *Discipleship*. Minneapolis, MN: Fortress Press.

FRANZ JÄGERSTÄTTER (1907-43)

Husband, Layman, Conscientious
Objector

In the last year of the Second Vatican Council (1962-65), a bishop spoke to the assembly about the life and death of a young unknown Austrian whose 1964 biography had just appeared in print. Archbishop Thomas Roberts, S.J., suggested that the church urge its members to say no, as this young man had done, when required by the state to commit sins or be part of a system steeped in injustice and lies. As a result, one of the council's key documents, Gaudium et Spes, *also known as the Pastoral Constitution on the Church in the Modern World, took a decisive stance against crimes that incurred the "indiscriminate destruction" of human life and spoke in favor of those renouncing "violence altogether, seeking a more just and compassionate society by nonviolent means." On October 26, 2007, this young man who had preferred death at the guillotine to taking the military oath of service in the Nazi Army was beatified by the church at the cathedral of Linz, Austria. Present were his widow, daughters, and numerous grandchildren, nieces, and nephews.*

Franz Jägerstätter was born on May 29, 1907, at St. Ra-

degund, Austria. His mother was Rosalia Huber, his father Franz Bachmeier, both of them farm helpers and unwed. They never married, perhaps because of parental opposition or because of the potential loss of employment for farm helpers who became married. The boy was raised by his grandmother. When the mother married the farmer Heinrich Jägerstätter in 1917, Franz was adopted by him and made heir to the estate. Between 1927 and 1931, Jägerstätter worked in the mining industry, oblivious to the church and somewhat extravagant; he had bought himself a motorcycle, the first in the village. In 1933, he fathered a child with Theresia Auer Kirsch. In 1935, he met Franziska Schwaninger, and they were married on the morning of Maundy Thursday in 1936. Instead of the typical wedding reception after the ceremony, the couple chose to board a train to Rome that same morning, spending their honeymoon as Easter pilgrims in the eternal city. The marriage calmed Jägerstätter's restlessness, not least for Franziska's deep Christian faith. Together, they prayed and read the scriptures at home and went to masses, vigils, and religious celebrations at the church in St. Radegund. In 1940, Jägerstätter became a tertiary in the order of St. Francis, a religious commitment to the evangelical counsels of poverty, chastity, and obedience in the context of marriage, the family, and the world. The following year, he volunteered his services as the sacristan at St. Radegund's church, which put him in charge of maintaining the altar decorations and flower beds, and of assisting the priest at weddings, funerals, and baptisms.

The couple's marriage was a happy one. Franziska called it "one of the happiest ones in our parish," so "people envied us." To her, Franz was "a good husband and an exemplary father for my children." Their daughter Rosalia had been born in 1937, Maria in 1938, and Aloisia in 1940. The couple was also prepared to adopt Jägerstätter's other child, Hildegard Auer, but they encountered resistance from her mother. Nonetheless, Hildegard was part of the family celebrations on holidays, and Jägerstätter meticulously met his paternal obligation of paying child support to Frau Kirsch.

The seventh-grade education he had received in the one-room village school did not prevent Jägerstätter from reading widely. Newspapers, religious devotionals, and church literature introduced him to the traditions of the early church, the lives of the saints and martyrs, papal encyclicals, and the currents of political and social thought. The depth of his biblical knowledge and his grasp of the scriptures—the gospels, in particular—along with his ability to put his thoughts in writing and to interpret current events in light of biblical passages is no less than astounding. His ability of relating the words of scripture to the contemporary life of faith led to his fateful step of refusing to take the oath of military combat, which would cost him his life.

Jägerstätter's refusal to serve "two masters," the Nazi regime and God, was the fruit of disciplined prayer and study. His faith became internalized; his listening sharpened to discern the voice of a conscience held captive by God. By 1938, Jägerstätter already showed clarity regarding his convictions. A national plebiscite should confirm what most Austrians favored: Austria would join the Third Reich under Hitler, making it become part of a "Greater Germany" through the so-called Anschluss. Jägerstätter let it be known that he would never serve the Nazis, casting the only no vote in the village. By doing so, he had gone against the majority opinion of his fellow citizens and the bishop's counsel in the form of a pastoral letter, read aloud throughout the diocese.

Between 1940 and 1941, Jägerstätter took military training and was brought up close to the war machinery and machinations of the Nazi regime. His resolve tightened not to *compromise his Christian faith by serving what he considered an evil leader, Hitler, and a warring state that was pillaging, ravaging, and destroying human lives. In February 1943, he was ordered to report for military duty. On March 2, he declared his refusal to take the oath of combat. On August 9, 1943, he was beheaded at Berlin, Tegel, as an "enemy of the state." For years, Franziska was refused both a widow's pension by the Austrian government and the villagers' sympathy over the loss of her husband and the father of her children.*

* * *

As required by state law, Jägerstätter reports on June 17, 1940, for military training at Braunau am Inn, Hitler's birthplace, and is sent from there to the military training center at Enns. His absence from the labor-intensive family farm is sorely felt. He is allowed to return home briefly for the Christmas holiday and again between late January and early February 1941. But not until April 21, 1941, is he being granted a military deferral in order to maintain the family farm. Upon his return, Jägerstätter becomes the sacristan at St. Radegund's church, where he also assists with weddings, funerals, and baptisms.

Dearest Fanj, I readily believe you when you say that your heart is often heavy, especially when Rosal always asks whether her father has come home yet. Tell her that when she is good about saying her prayers, then her father will return home. Indeed, it would be beautiful and right if I could be at home and remain there.

Yet I do not regret that I did not act differently. I reproach myself for only one thing, that everything here is actually going well. I did not know at the outset where I would end up and that the room and board here would be so excellent. In general, we do not even know whether it will be good for us when things go according to our wishes. Christ said that whoever wants to be my disciple must take up his cross and follow me (see Mark 8:34). I think about whether it would be much better if I had sought a deferral, and then I could have come home from Ried. But if I had, I would perhaps have to leave you now. Anxious rabbits want deferrals. I do not begrudge those who are able to remain at home. But we need not believe that those at home are so fortunate for they will be anxious every day. In the end, our current situation could be your lucky star.

Dear Fanj, consider this. If my entire life were to go well in all aspects of its physical well-being, I would notice nothing today about my life. I would not see that we have lived fortunate and harmonious years in our marriage. This good fortune is unforgettable and will accompany me through time and eternity. You also know how the children bring me joy. For this reason, a feeling of good fortune comes over me here so that tears of joy flow from my eyes when I think about our reunion.   — Enns, October 19, 1940

Dearest wife! Today I again gathered wealth for eternity. I was able to participate in a few Masses. We do not yet have a priest shortage in Enns, and one can find active Catholics among the soldiers. They are few in number, but they are not eradicated. It is really a joy when one meets Catholics who bear their fate entirely differently from the other men. Tomorrow we shall again travel to Steyr for sharpshooting practice. Hopefully, it will not be very cold, for one quickly gets cold standing around. Hopefully, too, the beautiful weather will at least partially continue until these days of training are over. When I am once again at home, then it can storm very often, and I'll not need to go out of the house. Or will you throw me outside? I'll hope for the best, and also Rosi will defend me, especially if I bring her more chocolate.

How is it going with the cutting of straw? Hopefully, the

animals are not eating too much of it. Have you greased the scythes and already hung them up? I'll end my letter now, for I want to go to Benediction and afterward drink one or two small glasses of beer.   —Enns, November 17, 1940

Dearest wife! Above all, receive my warm greetings. Today I can still write you from Enns. At 4 p.m., we shall apparently learn when we'll depart. For this reason I'll end my letter later tonight. I hope, dear Fanj, that you do not take this recent news too hard. In this difficult time one must be ready for anything. While it appears to us that my reassignment—instead of a leave or a discharge—is unfortunate, it may not in fact be so. It was on Friday, which is dedicated to the Sacred Heart of Jesus, that I received this sad news, and this feast cannot be a day of misfortune for us, at the very least in relation to eternal life. It need not be that everything in this world comes out as we want for ourselves, for we do not see the future. It is perhaps a good thing that we do not know it.

Dear Fanj, yesterday which was the feast of the Immaculate Conception, I was able to share in a Sunday of great grace. In the festively decorated Franciscan church amid a fine celebration, two soldiers were accepted into the Third Order. Dearest wife, one of these two soldiers was your husband. I hope that you are not upset with him for this, for you have—as I hope—the same view of life that I do. It must also be a consolation for you that my faith has not become weaker in the military. If I cannot be helpful to you in your work at home, I hope I can bring you help through my prayer.

          —Enns, December 9, 1940

In four notebooks kept from 1941 to 1943, Jägerstätter recorded questions and observations concerning Christian

discipleship, ethical principles for a Christian life, and delibera-
tions on the political, social, and ecclesiastical situation of the
time. In the second notebook, written in 1942, he recounted a
dream he had in 1938, the year when Austria joined the Third
Reich in the Anschluss by plebiscite. Prior to the dream, he
had read an article reporting that 150,000 young Austrians
had entered the Hitler Youth, hence joined the Nazi Party. The
Reich required all youth between the ages of ten and eighteen
to belong to the Hitler Youth.

I initially lay awake in bed until midnight, even though I was
not sick. Then I must have fallen asleep for at least a little while,
for I saw [in a dream] a wonderful train as it came around a
mountain. With little regard for the adults, the children flowed
to this train and were not held back. There were present a few
adults who did not go into the area. I do not want to give their
names nor describe them. Then a voice said to me, "This train
is going to hell." Immediately it happened that someone took
me by the hand, and the same voice said to me: "Now we are
going to purgatory." What I glimpsed and perceived was fearful.
If this voice had not told me that we were going to purgatory, I
would have judged that I had found myself in hell. Apparently,
only a few seconds passed during which I glimpsed all of this.
Then I heard a rushing sound and saw a light, and everything
went away. I immediately awoke my wife and recounted to
her everything that had transpired. . . .

It is now clear that this image represents nothing other than
National Socialism with all of its distinct organizations—the
N.S. German Workers' Party, the N.S. Public Assistance program, the N.S. Women's Association,, the Hitler Youth, and
so forth—that were breaking in or sneaking in at that time.
In other words, the train represents the N.S. *Volk* community
and everything for which it sacrifices and struggles. . . .

I believe that the German-speaking people never participated as strongly in Christian charitable activities as they are now engaging in the N.S. organizations. Nor were they as ready to contribute their money to church programs. . . .

Prior to Hitler's seizure of power [on January 30, 1933], many bishops in Germany banned National Socialists from receiving communion. But how is it now in the Reich? Many people who are members of the N.S. Party go to the communion rail with peace of mind. Also, their children participate in the Hitler Youth, or they receive instructions from N.S. teachers.

Have the National Socialists now—after more than two years of bringing about the horrible murders of people—adopted a new orientation that would allow and even promote the silence of church officials? Have church officials reached the decision that it is now permissible for Catholics to belong to a party that opposes the church? Have they given a positive evaluation of National Socialism?

An ordinary person would surely like to cry out at times. When one reflects even a little on these matters, one wonders whether those who are the most upright in our land are making a mistake. After all of the [church's] warnings, a bloody Christian persecution will not occur in our land because the church does almost everything that the N.S. party wants or commands.

Austria would no longer have many good priests in freedom or in their ministry if its Catholic clergy had stalwartly voted no in the plebiscite of April 10, 1938. Instead, church officials praised the N.S. Party for its many good acts and so helped generate 100 percent support for the N.S. state. Things would be no worse today for genuine Christian faith in our land if the churches were no longer open and if thousands of Christians had poured out their blood and their lives for Christ and their faith. This would have been better than now watching silently as there is more and more acceptance of falsehood. Yet many people are impatiently waiting for a liberation from this sad situation.

It would be worthwhile if we were to think about the Führer's words: "If you take care of yourself, then you are taking care of God." I would like to cry out to the people aboard the N.S. train: "Jump off this train before it arrives at your last stop, where you will pay with your life!" I believe that God has clearly spoken to me through this dream or appearance and placed it in my heart so that I could decide whether to be a National Socialist or a Catholic!

I am not throwing stones at our bishops and priests. They are human beings of flesh and blood as we are, and they can be weak. Perhaps they are even more tempted by the evil foe than we are. Perhaps, too, they were too little prepared to take on this struggle and to decide for themselves whether to live or to die. Would not our hearts shake [as theirs must have] if it were to come about that we would have to appear before God's judgment seat and be accountable for a decision that would affect so many other human beings? These thoughts help us appreciate more fully the difficult decision before which the bishops and priests stood in March 1938.

Perhaps our bishops thought that the new state would continue for only a short time and then fall apart and that by means of their accommodation they could spare many martyrs and much pain among believers. Unfortunately, things have gone otherwise. Many years have passed, and thousands of people die every year amid this falsehood. We can easily imagine what a heroic decision it would have been to have opposed what the N.S. state has demanded of the bishops during these recent years. Let's not reproach the bishops so that we make the situation more difficult for them than it already is. Rather, let us pray for them, asking that God enlighten them for the great challenge before which they still stand.

If we seriously observe the era in which we now live, we must conclude that the situation for us German-speaking Christians is far more hopeless and complex than it was for the Christians in the first centuries amid the bloody persecutions. Many will perhaps ask themselves, "Why has the Lord God allowed us to live in such a time?" We should not blame God, nor should we shift the blame to other people. The adage applies here: "Where we put ourselves to sleep is what we lie in." Still today it is possible with God's help—if we make serious efforts and apply all our strength—to get ourselves out of this swamp in which we are stuck and to become eternally blessed.

We must keep in mind, of course, that suffering during our earthly lives is not the worst thing. Even the saints had to suffer frightfully until God took them into eternal life. The Lord did not spare even his apostles from suffering, and most of them lost their lives through martyrdom. And the prospect of martyrdom did not deter them from working so much for Christ.

Amid our sinful lives, we want to live without suffering and struggles, to have a gentle death, and to attain eternal well-being beyond all of this. Christ himself, the most blameless individual, suffered the most among all human beings and purchased heaven for us by means of his suffering and death. Yet we do not want to suffer for him! If we study history and look into the past centuries, we are not surprised that we are in this situation today. Over the years, a deep and devout faith has increasingly receded, and a new paganism has increasingly pushed ahead. Centuries ago, the good writers of religious history said—indeed, some even predicted—that great misery would come upon human beings if they did not improve themselves.

We need only look at Russia. What great suffering among the

people! When will they be liberated from it? Should everything be painless for us now as many people hold?

    —"One Today's Issue: Catholic or National Socialist," FJ, pp. 173-76.

Adam and Eve completely ruined their destiny by their disobedience against God [Genesis 3]. They would not have suffered if they had obeyed God rather than the seducer. Also, God could have directed their thoughts differently. . . .

"Are Austria and Bavaria blameless in that we now have a N.S. state instead of a Christian one? Did National Socialism simply fall on us from the sky?" I believe that in response we need not waste many words. Whoever was not asleep during the last one hundred years knows well enough how and why everything has come about.

I believe that what happened in the spring of 1938 was not much different from what happened on Holy Thursday more than nineteen hundred years ago when [Pilate] gave the Jewish people a free choice between the blameless Savior and the thief Barabbas. At that time, the Pharisees had even handed out money among the people so that they would cry out and also so that they would lead astray and intimidate those who still followed Christ. What did some people allege and fabricate against Christian-oriented Chancellor Schuschnigg and against the clergy, even engaging in support for blood-curdling marches? The few people who did not err and did not give the unfortunate yes [in the plebiscite] were simply called fools or communists. Even today, some people have not relinquished their campaigns against these "fools" in order to win them over to the N.S. *Volk* community or at least to have them give up their ideas! Clearly the joy of victory has not lasted long among many people, and many of these people have come to recognize that things are now quite different from what was promised at the outset. Yet the situation today has not disgusted them nor caused them to revolt. They do not have the courage to separate themselves from this anti-Christian *Volk* community. . . .

If it is to happen in our wonderful Austria that Christ is again to reign, then a Good Friday must come after a Holy Thursday. Christ must first die before he can rise again from the dead. There will be no resurrection for us if we are not ready to suffer and, if need be, even to die for Christ and our faith. . . .

I believe that the Lord God does not make it difficult for us to give over our lives for our faith. We need only think that already thousands of young men have been summoned [by the state] to make their lives available in this difficult time of war, and many have already sacrificed their youthful lives [in combat]. So outsiders, who have occupied our homeland and stolen our goods, are able to demand the lives of our young men and to extinguish the souls of thousands of our children. Our awareness of our guilt as German-speaking people gets increasingly greater with every new victory that we attain for Germany. Why should it be so hard to give up our lives for a king [i.e., Christ] who imposes important obligations on us but also gives us rights, whose ultimate victory is certain, and whose kingdom exists forever? By his harsh suffering and earthly death, Christ has redeemed us from eternal death but not from earthly suffering and death. Christ demands from us also a public acknowledgment of our faith, exactly as the Führer Adolf Hitler demands from his *Volk*.

God's Commandments teach us that we have to be obedient to our worldly authorities, even if they are not Christian, but only insofar as they command us to do something that is not morally wrong. We must still obey God more than we obey human beings. And who can serve two masters at once? [see Matt. 6:24].

—"Brief Thoughts on Our Past, Present, and Future,"
FJ, pp. 177-80.

Are we perhaps able to bring about a conversion in others when we—in order to attain some kind of favorable appraisal—apparently do everything that the N.S. Party wants from us or orders us to do? What must people of other beliefs think about us and about our Christian belief when we value it so little? We must bring shame on ourselves among true N.S. Party members who made personal sacrifices for their N.S. ideals [prior to 1938], who suffered for the N.S. worldview despite the laws against National Socialism at that time. They were not intimated by imprisonment and death, though their faith concerned earthly goals. Would they have attained their victories if they had been cowardly and fearful as we German-speaking Catholics are today? We German-speaking Catholics hope to bring about a glorious victory for our Christian faith without a struggle and want to accomplish this victory after we first struggle on behalf of our N.S. opponents and help them become victorious.

May we reflect on this strategy? I believe that the world has never experienced something similar to this. Humankind is surely very smart and inventive today. But has it ever found that one group of people can be victorious over another without a struggle? I have never heard of such a thing!

—"A Game of Deceit," FJ, pp. 185.

Some people say that others bear the responsibility for our wrongful acts, that our civil and ecclesiastical officials bear great responsibility [for what is happening]. However, instead of making the burden of responsibility lighter for these officials, some people want to place the guilt on them—the guilt that these people themselves could easily bear and that would implicate them deeply in things! Do our officials actually bear great responsibility before God as we sometimes believe, or have we lost our sense of responsibility as others sometimes tell us and as we may often tell ourselves?

Will not God judge every human being in relation to his or her own self-understanding rather than in relation to the position or office that the person has held? . . . .

In my judgment, people bear more guilt for their actions when they fully recognize that these actions are more bad than good and when they nevertheless do them so that no danger and no deprivations will afflict their pampered bodies. (Of course, these people find sweet words that their actions are the responsibility of other people.) These people bear more guilt than those people who simply do what they do because they see their actions as their duty and, according to their thinking, entirely good.

—"On the Loss of Responsibility," FJ, pp. 186-87.

If it were only a war about land as so many others have been and if Germany were actually to end up as the victor, then Catholics at the end of this war would possess the same rights as every other citizen in the German Reich. But if this war is in fact a revolution or a conflict about religious belief, then I could fight for the N.S. Reich as much as I want and yet I—despite all of the exertions and sacrifice that I as a poor soldier had offered—would be seen at the war's end as Austrian Christians are seen today, even though they submitted themselves—not freely—four years ago to the National Socialists.

These thoughts alone suffice for someone not to fight for this state or for the N.S. *Volk* community. Further, I believe that many people have forgotten what the Holy Father said about National Socialism in his encyclical many years ago, namely, that National Socialism is even more dangerous than Communism. Since Rome has not withdrawn this judgment, I believe that it is not likely a crime or a sin if someone as a Catholic were to refuse the current obligation for military service—even though a person who refuses military service is surely looking at death. Is it more Christian for someone to give himself as a sacrifice than to have to murder others who possess a right to life on earth and who want to live in order to save their lives for a short while?

—"War or Revolution," FJ, pp. 189-90.

To lead souls to Christ is one of the most wonderful tasks to which God more or less ultimately calls all of us. It is sad in our current situation that we laity are not able to rescue a few more souls. We look on helplessly as close relatives and many souls, for whom we bear responsibility, are drowning in this stream in which all of us are now swimming. We may not even advise them on how they could be rescued from it. Yet we laity would be able to give some of them necessary advice on how to make it to the other river bank. Our spiritual leaders, on whom we rely the most and should rely, now remain silent. Or they tell some of us even the opposite of what we should do if we are to be rescued from this dangerous stream. As long as they do this, it is of course better that we laity remain entirely silent. If people are already weak and find themselves bewildered, we could lead them into even greater bewilderment through our advice.

As long as our priests and bishops are giving us no advice about the dangerous situation in which almost all of us are finding ourselves or are offering us poor advice, we laity must at best pray to God that he allow us to succeed in reaching the other river bank as soon as possible. So other people can at least see and perhaps follow the example of how this person or that person has been fortunately rescued on the other river bank.

—"We Should Be Lay Apostles," FJ, p. 198.

From the third notebook, written between late 1942 and early 1943; the notebook contains seven questions and a response to each, which Jägerstätter may have used to help him prepare for the anticipated interrogations by the military officials.

6. In the past it often happened that a city or an entire nation would allow its moral character to decline quite low. Then some citizens would rise up and try to save what could still be saved. The just people among these citizens would feel compelled to make atonement, and the formerly unjust people among them would seek to do penance. But what do we hear today about atonement and penance? . . . .

Today we frequently hear people say that we can do nothing more and that if we were to say something, we would find ourselves in prison or dead. They add that we cannot change much in world events. However, did things go much for our missionaries who often brought about no results other than the reward of their own imprisonment or death?

I perceive that many words will not accomplish much today. Words teach, but personal example shows their meaning. Even if we are as silent as a wall, we can nevertheless do much good. People want to observe Christians who have taken a stand in the contemporary world, Christians who live amid all of the darkness with clarity, insight, and conviction, Christians who live with the purest peace of mind, courage, and dedication amid the absence of peace and joy, amid the self-seeking and the hatred. People are looking for Christians who are not like a wavering reed that is pushed back and forth by every light breeze, for Christians who ask primarily about the teaching of Christ and our faith, Christians who do not watch to see how their associates will respond to this or that point. If signposts are set in the ground so loosely that they can be turned by every wind and, as a result, point in this direction and then in that direction, is someone for whom the way is unfamiliar able to find the right path?   —FJ, p. 211.

In February 1943, Jägerstätter was asked to report at Enns for military duty. Certain that he would not return, he bid farewell to his wife, children, and mother. On March 1, he walked into the induction center, but due to overcrowding had to come back the next day. On March 2, Jägerstätter declared to the military officials his refusal to do military duty, was arrested and incarcerated from March 2 to May 4 at Linz, then taken by train to a prison in Berlin, Tegel. In a letter from Linz sent via a cellmate who was being released, he was able to speak openly about the reports he heard from other inmates and his joy of hearing of those "who are not being pulled along by the crowd."

Dearest wife! First of all, my warmest greetings. Since this letter will leave here this morning with a cellmate who is being released, it will come to you without being censored. I want to write a few sentences to you. Perhaps you will receive a visit from this fellow who was in our cell and will go free today.

You should not give any testimony to anyone. I advise you to say only one thing if someone asks you whether you agree with my decision not to fight. Honestly say how it has been most difficult for you. I believe that you cannot lighten things for me.

I have no great terror before the lying and cheating [of N.S. officials]. If I did, I would not be sitting here. I want to save my life but not through lies. Officers in Enns wanted to trap me by means of trick questions and so to make me once again into a soldier. It was not easy to stick with my decision. It may become even more difficult. But I trust in God to let me know if it would be better for me to do something different.

I was of course asked what the pastor had said. I had to remain silent concerning his words, however, or he would no longer be free. So I calmly said that he had advised me to report for military service so that then I would do what's best. One comes to saying this when one considers what it would mean for a priest if one were to say something when asked about the priest's words.

I want also to tell you that there is a farm woman in Enns who has not allowed her children to join the H[itler] Y[outh]. This is a rarity. Yet one does hear that there are people in other places who are not being pulled along by the crowd. I want to say further that I hope that in this cell I shall have a greater awareness than I would have in the army. There are many men here to be comforted. One encounters here bitter disillusioned men. I am with men who broke various kinds of laws. What all of them recount is horrible. What people have gone through over these five years and what they have suffered [is terrible]! For the slightest offense, people are imprisoned for months. But months and years [of possible imprisonment] are reduced if one agrees to combat duty on the front. What does one offer to people with bitter disillusionments? If they would undergo conversion, it would be appropriate. There are SS men who have undergone a conversion before dying.

Give my greetings to our pastor, and tell him people are not often as bad as one may believe. However, they err because of religious ignorance. The pastor should give the greatest energy to Christian teachings, even when the attendance is lacking and when the effects seem empty. In any case, he will save his soul [by teaching the faith].

Warm greetings to you, your husband.

—Linz, March 5, 1943

Greetings in God! Dearest wife!

I arrived safely in Berlin on May 4 at 11 p.m. If it had been a vacation, it would have indeed been a lovely train ride, for the farms and villages through which we traveled were indeed extremely beautiful. Although I am removed farther from you, have no heavy heart because of me, for you know under what [divine] protection I exist.

Moreover, all goes well for me here. To be sure, it is a little different in some ways than at Linz, as far as I can now see. As at Linz, a person here need not suffer from hunger, and I find many things better here. In my cell, I have a very nice small closet of my own. It is surely not difficult for me that I had to come here. God does not want us to be lost, but fortunately to be with him in eternity. If one has vindictiveness against no one and can forgive all people, if one dismisses an occasional harsh word, then one's heart remains at peace. There is nothing more beautiful in this world than peace. So we pray to God that a true and lasting peace will soon move into the world.

—Berlin, Tegel, May 7, 1943

I continue to find my situation very satisfactory. My stomach is sometimes a bit of a rascal, but otherwise I feel healthy, thank God. My stomach's small disturbances are easy to put up with, for it could easily be worse. Otherwise, it is in all things better here for me than at Linz. I am still alone in my cell. Almost daily we have half-an-hour to move about freely. Also, one can work in his cell as much as he wants, making envelopes for [military] letters. It would surely be better for me if I could lessen your difficult work. This free choice is not possible since nothing has changed. At least I can still pray for you. It is also a grace of God when one can suffer for his faith. Here I can make the most beautiful retreat. If I were at home, I would give myself hardly a week for this time which means that I would keep putting it off.

About the future I still cannot tell you anything. Perhaps in the next letter. On May 24, I appeared before the Reich's Military Tribunal for interrogation. It was a somewhat long ride by car because the Tribunal is in Berlin itself, and Tegel is somewhat outside the city. On the way, I caught a small glimpse of the vastness of the city.

You must be already busy with the haying. Will Rosl and Maridl already be helpful in this? Hopefully, you received more rain there in May than we did here. Otherwise, it will be likely disastrous for the fruit. You can imagine that it was painful for me [to hear] about the beautiful May devotions. As a substitute for them, I held a May devotion every day in my cell at night. In place of a statue of Mary, I used the dried violet from Rosl that you sent me. Surely it is more beautiful when a father can join with his entire family in the devotion. Let us pray in this month to the Sacred Heart of Jesus that he will soon bring peace to the world when all people also want it. The month of June is one of the most beautiful months of the church year.

Dearest wife, if it is God's will, there will still occur in this life an opportunity for us to have a reunion. I believe that each of us longs for this. Be at peace! Let us love one another and readily forgive each other. Most people embitter their lives by their lack of reconciliation.

Frau Kirsch wrote to me. I should send her a confirmation of my military unit so that she will receive her benefits. She apparently received my address from you. I do not know where the whole thing stands and whether it is still paid to her. If it is possible, I would ask you, dear wife, to pay her for the time being. One does not know how things will work after my case is decided and whether she will receive something from the state. . . .

And now, my dear children, have you forgotten your father because he has not written you for a long time and has not come home? You are once again picking strawberries and blueberries. Soon you will be looking for cherries at Lang's.

Loisie is already haying. If you are well behaved and obedient children, then the loving God will make everything right again.

I warmly greet you, my dearest wife, as well as mother and my dear little ones. Your father, husband, and son, Franz.

—Berlin, June 6, 1943

On July 6, the Reich's Tribunal condemned Jägerstätter to death, a fact he did not mention in his letter written two days later and addressed to his wife, mother, father-in-law, and children. Rather, he reported his joy over a visit from a priest, a prison chaplain. Jägerstätter did not mention that the priest had shared with him the story of a Tyrolean priest, Franz Reinisch, whom the Reich had executed on August 21, 1942, because of the priest's refusal to take the military oath. Later, the visiting priest, Heinrich Kreutzberg, recalled the calm that had come over Jägerstätter when hearing Reinisch's story, most certainly a confirmation of Jägerstätter's own "solitary witness."

It is a joy to be able to suffer for Jesus and our faith. We have the joyful hope that the few days in this life when we have been separated will be replaced by thousands of days in eternity, where we shall rejoice with God and our heavenly Mother in untroubled joy and good fortune. If we can only remain in the love of God when difficult tests of our faith come to us. We do not know in this life whether we are spoken of when it says that the most righteous will be saved. . . .

Dear mother, thank you for your sentences, which have delighted me. I hope that you are no longer angry with me for my disobedience. I also ask that you not be concerned about my physical well-being. If something difficult were to come upon me, it would not matter. The loving God will not send me more than I can bear. . . .

All of you are interested in knowing whether my future has yet been decided. Please be patient until my next letter. I hope to include something then about the final decision.

Dearest wife, for a long time I have been very fortunate. You need have no heavy heart about me. Do not forget me in your prayers as I am not forgetting you. Remember me especially during the Holy Sacrifice of the Mass. I can share my joy with you that yesterday a priest visited me. Next Tuesday he will come with the Blessed Sacrament. One is not abandoned by God here.   —Tegel, July 8, 1943

At the request of Jägerstätter's defense attorney, his wife, and their pastor at St. Radegund, Ferdinand Fürthauer, came to visit him in the Berlin prison. Jägerstätter did not know of their coming. During the visit on July 13, 1943, which the prison guards cut short to only twenty minutes' time, the pastor asked him, on the advice of the defense attorney, to sign a statement saying he would serve in the army. Jägerstätter became annoyed with him and refused. Both his wife and Pastor Fürthauer returned to Austria the same day.

Dearest wife, you once again made a great sacrifice for me [by coming here]. Tomorrow it will be four weeks since we saw each other. It would have saved you much pain if my defense attorney had not written to you. I still have not received a statement that my death sentence has been reconfirmed. You must offer to God your effort and great expense [in coming here], which would not otherwise have come about [if the defense attorney had not contacted you].

To be sure, I received great joy from our reunion, but not from the fact that you had to make such a great sacrifice. It brought me pain that I could speak so briefly with you. I am not angry with the pastor. I have asked his forgiveness for all of my unnecessary words to him, which perhaps hurt him and only brought me regret. I did not want to bring pain with my words, just as the pastor did not want to do so with his. I wanted to spare you this suffering that you have borne for me.

However, you know Christ's words: "Whoever comes to me and does not hate father and mother, wife and children, brothers and sisters, yes, even life itself, cannot be my disciple" [Luke 14:26]. How it must have brought Christ much heartache as he inflicted pain on his mother through his suffering, which is not comparable with our suffering! And Jesus endured all of this only out of love for us sinners.

Do you believe that all would go well with me if I were to tell a lie in order to prolong my life? I sensed your pain in your words about me sinning against the Fourth Commandment. How our final hours will be, we do not know. Nor do we know what struggles we must still pass through. That I have great trust in God's compassion, that my dear Savior will not abandon me in the final hours—who has not abandoned me up until now—this you can believe with me. Our dear heavenly Mother will also not [abandon me], for not a few "Hail Marys" flow from my lips. This you can also consider.

Dearest wife, consider what Jesus has promised to those who make the Nine First Fridays. Everything will become clear on the Day of Judgment, if not sooner, as to why so many people are struggling today. With my heart, I apologize to you and to everyone else if some of these words that reach your ears are not kind. Did our dear Savior not mean everything? And should we be exempted from his words? For the riches of eternity will not be less if I am defamed by many people. The chief thing is only that the Lord not be ashamed of me for eternity. God the Lord wants to come to us in our final hours, not as our Judge but as our Redeemer.

Do not be overly concerned about earthly things. The Lord indeed knows what we need as long as we are pilgrims in this world. When so much can change and so much goes differently from what we would like, we know nevertheless what we can atone for here on this earth. In the next life we need suffer no longer. And the greater the suffering here, the greater the joy there. —Tegel, August 8, 1943

Between his death verdict and his execution, Jägerstätter wrote on odd pieces of paper five essays on his refusal of unconditional obedience to Hitler, prompted in part by the brief meeting with his wife and his pastor. Jägerstätter's handwriting is uncharacteristically small, meaning probably that he was already wearing handcuffs at the time of writing. The last essay, identified as Text no. 88, was given by Franziska Jägerstätter on loan to the memorial exhibit of modern martyrs in Rome's San Bartolomeo Church.

Now I'll write down a few words as they come to me from my heart. Although I am writing them with my hands in chains, this is still much better than if my will were in chains.

God sometimes shows his power, which he wishes to give to human beings, to those who love him and do not place earthly matters ahead of eternal ones. Not prison, not chains, and not even death are capable of separating people from the love of God, or robbing them of their faith and free will [see Rom. 8:31-39]. God's power is invincible.

"Be obedient, and submit to authority." These words are flying today at a person from all sides, especially from people who no longer believe anything that exists in Sacred Scripture and that God has commanded us to believe. If someone were to concern himself with what these people are saying, then he would assume that heaven is in fact in this world. For instead of being concerned about saving me from serious sins and directing me toward eternal life, these people are concerned about rescuing me from an earthly death.

They always want to prick my conscience concerning my responsibilities for my wife and children. Is the action that someone does somehow morally better because this person is married and has children? Or is the action better or worse because thousands of other Catholics are doing? Has smoking a cigarette also become a virtue because thousands of Catholics are doing it? Is someone permitted to lie in taking an oath just because he has a wife and children? Did not Christ himself say that whoever loves wife, mother and children more than me is not worthy of me? [see Luke 14:26]. On what basis do we ask God for the Seven Gifts of the Holy Spirit if we should adhere to blind obedience in any case?

For what purpose did God create all human beings with intelligence and free will if it is not our place—as many are now saying—to decide whether this war, which Germany is conducting, is just or unjust? For what purpose does someone need to recognize the difference between good and evil?

I believe that someone can calmly adhere to blind obedience only when one will surely not harm anyone else. If people were totally honest today—as some Catholics are, I believe—they would have to say, "Yes, I see that the acts that I am required to do are not morally good, but I am simply not ready to die [for refusing to do them]."

If God had not bestowed on me the grace and power to die for my faith—if this is demanded of me—then I would be doing the same as the majority of people are doing. God can give someone as much grace as God wants. If other men and women had received as much grace as I have obtained, they would have perhaps done much more good than I have done.

—Text no. 88, FJ, pp. 243-44.

Jägerstätter wrote his last letter to his family and loved ones from the Brandenburg prison on August 9. On that day the verdict was to be confirmed at 2 p.m. and carried out at 4 p.m. Jägerstätter was indeed beheaded at 4 p.m. on August 9. Unaware of the day and hour of her husband's death, Franziska had felt to be in personal communion with her husband at that time, a sense so strong that she had made a mental note of it.

I want to write all of you a few words of farewell. Dearest wife and mother, I am deeply grateful for everything that you have done for me in my life, for all of the love and sacrifices which you have shown me. And I ask you once again to forgive me for everything that I have made you suffer and feel hurt. You have surely been forgiven by me for everything. I ask everyone else, whom I at some time may have pained and hurt, to forgive me. Especially the pastor if I have perhaps hurt him with my words as he visited with me. I forgive everyone from my heart. May God accept my life as a sin offering not merely for my sins but also for others' sins [see 4 Macc. 6:28-29].

Dearest wife and mother, it was not possible for me to free both of you from the sorrows that you have suffered for me. How hard it must have been for our dear Lord that he had given his dear mother such great sorrow through his suffering and death! And she suffered everything out of love for us sinners. I thank our Savior that I could suffer for him and may die for him. I trust in his infinite compassion. I trust that God forgives me everything and will not abandon me in the last hour.

Dearest wife, consider what Jesus has promised to those who make the Nine First Fridays. Also, consider that Jesus will come to me in Holy Communion and strengthen me for the journey into eternity. In Tegel prison, I received the grace of the Blessed Sacrament four times.

Give my warm greetings to my dear children. If I am soon in

heaven, I shall ask the loving God to prepare a place for all of you. Over the past weeks, I have prayed often to the heavenly Mother that if it is God's will that I die soon, that I celebrate the feast of Mary's Assumption in heaven.

—Brandenburg, August 9, 1943

SOURCES

Jägerstätter, Franz. 2009. *Letters and Writings from Prison.* Edited by Erna Putz. Maryknoll, NY: Orbis Books.

Alfred Delp, S.J.
(1907-45)

*Pastor and Collaborator
in the Kreisau Circle*

*Eight days after the unsuccessful attempt on Hitler's life on
July 20, 1944, two Gestapo officials were waiting for a Jesuit
priest to finish morning mass before arresting him on charges
of treason. Taken straight from the church's rectory in Munich to a prison in Berlin, the priest would spend the next six
months handcuffed and in solitary confinement, being repeatedly beaten, tortured, and interrogated. While awaiting trial
at the Tegel prison, and in the face of death, he began making
notes on the meaning of the incarnation, Christ's death and
resurrection, and the way of living a fully surrendered life
for Christ. Two years after his execution by hanging in 1945,
his letters and prison meditations on Advent smuggled out
by friends were first published in German, and in 1963, they
were published in English with an introduction by Thomas
Merton. Today, they are considered one of the great classics of
Christian literature.*

*Alfred Delp was born on September 15, 1907, in Mannheim,
the second of six children of the unwed Johann Adam Friedrich Delp, a Lutheran, and Maria Bernauer, a Catholic. They
married shortly after his birth. Though baptized a Catholic,*

Delp was raised Lutheran and confirmed. A falling out with the Lutheran pastor led him to transfer church membership to a Catholic parish, whose pastor had been looking after the family in the absence of the father during World War I, and to leave the Lutheran school for a diocesan-run Catholic school in Dieburg. After completing his secondary education at a classical German gymnasium, Delp entered the Jesuit novitiate at Feldkirch, Austria, in 1926. It is there that he first became acquainted with the young theologian and Jesuit Karl Rahner, who had been brought in as a Latin teacher and who would later call Delp "a good friend of mine." In 1935, Delp published a critical study of the philosophy of Martin Heidegger, titled Tragic Existence. *That same year, he also planned on a collaborative work with several Jesuits, both Rahner and Hans Urs von Balthasar among them, that would engage National Socialism and propose an alternate society based on Christian principles. Titled by Delp* The Reconstruction, *the book remains only in outline form, since the collaborative effort never materialized.*

Ordained to the priesthood in 1937 at the Jesuit church of St. Michael in Munich (the same church where Rahner had been ordained five years earlier), Delp was granted permission by his order to pursue doctoral studies in social philosophy. But the Nazi administrator of the University of Munich denied him admission, so Delp joined the staff of the Jesuit cultural monthly Stimmen der Zeit *("Voices of These Times"), becoming editor for social and political thought. When in 1941 the Nazis shut down the magazine, Delp was assigned by his superiors to serve as rector of the small St. Georg's church in Bogenhausen, a suburb of Munich. In addition to pastoral care and saying mass, he would help repair damages to parishioners' homes caused by the ongoing bombing raids. He also aided Jews in their escape to Switzerland by collecting food and money for them, and was vocal, both from the pulpit and at Catholic gatherings, about the evils of National Socialism.*

The work in the parish helped Delp flesh out his vision concerning a new social order, the role of the church in it, and the task of the Christian, especially in light of oppression, the exploitation of labor, and injustice. Delp called this vision the Third Idea, writing on it an eighty-page manuscript that, unfortunately, has been lost. For Delp, people in the Western world were being tossed to and fro between two extreme worldviews: that of an individualistic, self-seeking materialism resulting in capitalism; and that of a collectivist Bolshevism that reduced the person to a mere number and resulted in communism. A third way had to be found. Delp's Third Idea was to develop an economic system that would supersede and synthesize the ideas of both capitalism and communism along the lines of socialist thought. Delp saw the papal social encyclicals as the foundation for such an alternative system. He himself had become an expert in matters of the social question and, in particular, on the anniversary encyclical Quadragesimo Anno (Fortieth Year), promulgated by Pope Pius XI in 1931, which suggested a Christian alternative to communism. In a book titled The Human Being and History *("Der Mensch und die Geschichte"), published in 1943, Delp elaborated on the existing tension between the eternal and the temporal orders at whose intersection always stood the human being and, in the final analysis, the God-man, Jesus Christ. This meant for Delp that Western society had no other alternative of a peaceful, harmonious coexistence but by seeing to the creation of a social order at whose center stood God in Christ.*

Through his own Jesuit provincial in Munich, Augustin Rösch (1893-1961), Delp was introduced to a secret resistance group, founded by the prominent and highly respected Count Helmuth James von Moltke (1907-45). Since 1941, members met on Moltke's estate at Kreisau in Lower Silesia—hence the group's name, Kreisau Circle. By then, the Nazi regime had succeeded in intimidating and terrorizing the German population to such a degree that most Germans felt paralyzed by fear and apathy. Moltke was looking beyond the present; with the help of experts in various fields, including theologians such as Dietrich Bonhoeffer, he planned for the time after the demise of Hitler's Third Reich, a time when the German nation could be rebuilt on the basis of Christian principles and under a new constitution. When Moltke was looking for an expert on social labor issues, Rösch suggested Delp, who readily agreed, while fully aware that such an involvement, if discovered by the Nazis, would mean certain death. Operating in Munich, Berlin, and Kreisau, the circle had as its members some of the nation's most educated and best-trained minds. With the failed attack on Hitler by the chief of staff of the general army office in Berlin, Count Claus Schenk von Stauffenberg (1907-44), the full range of the Kreisau connection came to light, along with an extensive list of names, Delp's included. Though not aware of the planned attack, Delp's involvement with a resistance group, along with his refusal to leave the Jesuit order in exchange for freedom, made him automatically a traitor of the Third Reich and an enemy of the state.

His six-month imprisonment would become for Delp a time of agony and of momentous transformation. Delp's confrontational and argumentative nature, which he regularly exercised in conversation, his tendency to excess and extravagance (he chain-smoked cigars), his proud swagger and intellectual arrogance did not go unobserved by classmates, confreres, and acquaintances. The provincial, too, surely noticed these characteristics in Delp and may have taken them into account in his decision to have Delp's vows postponed, though the order's records remain sealed as to the exact reason. By Delp's own testimony from prison, a change took place in him; a sense of surrender occurred, along with a previously unknown experience of the mercy and love of God. When on December 8, 1944, Delp was finally permitted to make his final profession of vows in the Society of Jesus under the watch of a prison guard, he was overcome by such awe that his words were punctuated by sobs. On January 23, 1945, Helmuth von Moltke was executed, along with the rest of the imprisoned members of the Kreisau group, except for Delp. On February 2, 1945, Delp was hanged at the Plötzensee prison, leaving behind in his cell a broken pair of eyeglasses, a rosary, and Thomas à Kempis's The Imitation of Christ.

* * *

Six weeks prior to his arrest, Delp had rushed to a house that had been heavily bombed. To his sorrow, he found there the body of Maria Urban, known as "Urbi," who had been the head teacher of the kindergarten attached to St. Georg's and a good friend. Three days later, a friend of Urbi's handed Delp a letter Urbi had written a full sixteen months earlier. In the letter Urbi wrote that realizing his important and dangerous work in resisting the Nazi regime and the constant danger to his life, she had asked God to take her life, instead, so Delp might be able to continue his work. Urbi's self-giving sacrifice continued to be a source of hope during Delp's imprisonment. Shortly after arriving at Tegel prison (Dietrich Bonhoeffer would be there as well but was kept in a different wing of the prison and transferred to the prison of the Gestapo headquarters in Berlin on October 8, 1944), Delp wrote to Marianne Hapig and Marianne Pünder, both workers in the resistance movement and known for helping political prisoners and their families. A friend to whom Delp had whispered the name "Hapig" while descending the train in Berlin had contacted Marianne Hapig,

*and both women had tracked Delp down at Moabit prison,
in Berlin; henceforth, they would become his only lifeline to
the outside world. By taking his laundry and returning them
in a basket at the Tegel prison, to which Delp was transferred
shortly thereafter, the two "Mariannes" were able to smuggle
in and out of prison Delp's letters and writings.*

*A letter from Tegel prison to the two Mariannes, September
30, 1944.*

Good people,

Many thanks for getting my clothes to me in such a moth-
erly way. And who would have thought that our holiday ac-
quaintance would have been forced to bring forth such fruit?
Please get me, if possible, a decent pair of shoes and a head
covering (size 54-55) so that I can take my daily hour outside,
even when it rains, etc. Greetings to my mother and everyone
in Munich. And every day remind Urbi of her word. She has
to keep it now. All the best and many thanks.

    Alfred Delp

P.S. I'd almost forgotten the most important thing. I'm in
Tegel Prison while investigations are going on for the People's
Court. I'd never dreamed this could be happening. I think it's
about time you looked for a lawyer for me. I know too few
people here. In Munich I heard the names of Dix and Peter
Schmitz mentioned. Be kind enough to give it some thought.

    Thanks for everything.

    Alfred Delp

*A letter to Luise Oestreicher, the secretary at St. Georg's in
Munich, end of October 1944. Not all the letters were dated
by Delp for security reasons and many of them were unsigned*

or signed with a pseudonym, such as Georg (from St. Georg's Church), Max, or Bullus, a nickname from his days at the Jesuit high school Stella Matutina, where he had taught in his early years as a Jesuit.

Dear L.

I'm back writing you a few greetings again. I don't know if they'll get to you. Actually, I know nothing about anyone except for the people handcuffed here, who are becoming fewer every day. "Unicus et pauper sum ego," or "I've become very alone and miserable," it says in the psalm. I'm so grateful for the Host, which I've had in my cell since October 1. It breaks the isolation, although, I'm ashamed to admit, sometimes I feel so tired and devastated that I can no longer grasp this reality at all.

Right now I need all my strength to cope with a toothache and the pain of sinus infection. I hope it won't fester. That's always been a nasty problem for me.

I can't write much to you today; it's not a good day. Sometimes one's whole destiny pushes itself together into a tonweight and settles on the heart, and one really doesn't know how long this heart can be expected to take it.

I've still heard nothing from you. That's also very hard at the moment. How can all this go on?

I believe in God and in life. And whatever we pray for with faith, we'll get. Faith is the secret. And I don't believe that God will let me choke. . . . But I honestly can't say anything better than that about my situation. God has profoundly entrapped me and challenged me to keep my word from former times: with him alone can one live and deal with one's destiny.

How is everything with you? Greetings to all the dear ones. Wishing you God's blessing and fulfillment.

Georg

I'd appreciate a few Masses at St. Georg's, if that's possible. At any rate, I must now rely on the community of good people. My own strength has gone. "God alone suffices": I said that once when I was very self-sufficient. And look at me now. Until now I did everything in a false manner, and it got increasingly worse. So tell Tattenbach and Dold to pray hard in the Society [of Jesus]. There's just nothing more they can do. If I were worth millions, some people would be able to get all the way to the top on my behalf, but I'm only a beaten and failed human being. May the walk across the tightrope be taken in God's name. Greetings to your family and to Johannes.

Also to Karl, Wessling, Laplace, Kessler, Chrysolia, Annemarie. Please send me news of the attacks.

To Luise Oestreicher, November 17, 1944

Dear L.

The decisive hour is inevitably creeping up. The possibility of a settlement beforehand has been cut off short. As things stand now, the hearing will be December 7 or 8. God has until then to work his miracle.

This week has in many ways been really turbulent. Three of our number have gone the way that remains a bitter possibility for all of us and from which only a miracle of God can separate and protect us. Inside myself, I have much to do, to ask, to offer up completely, before God. One thing is clear and tangible to me in a way that it seldom has been: the world is full of God. From every pore, God rushes out to us, as it were. But we're often blind. We remain stuck in the good times and the bad times and don't experience them right up to the point where the spring flows forth from God. That's true . . . for pleasant experiences as well as for unhappy ones. In everything, God wants to celebrate encounter and asks for the prayerful response of surrender. The trick and the duty is only this: to develop a lasting awareness and a lasting attitude out of these insights and graces—or rather, to allow them to develop. Then life becomes free, in that freedom which we have often looked for. . . .

I've just heard about the recent attacks in Munich. Please let me know how you and the friends are. It's really too much, this worry and uncertainty, on top of everything else.

Today is another hard day. God is dealing so intensely with me that he's making me rely on him totally. I've been in isolation now for some time. I should learn what believing and trusting mean. Every hour it's as if I'm learning this for the first time. There are also some good hours of fullness and comfort, but for the most part we're without any doubt on a tightrope and we have to walk across an abyss; and not only that, but snipers are shooting at us. And some of us are constantly falling off.

Some days I tell God that I'm a little bambino and I need some candy for comfort. He then responds to me in terrific ways. Recently, on one of these days the two Mariannes were able to get me twenty cigarettes and five cigars all at one time. And in the same way, the dear gray prayer book and a few things that tasted keenly of Munich. And sometimes I pray for a word of guidance and consolation, and so I break open the Scripture at random. I've just now opened it: Those who believe will do the following miracles. . . . Mark 16:16ff. I tried it again, like a game, and this time it broke open at Matthew 20. Another word of confidence.

Oh, how restricted is the human heart in matters of its own ability: in hope and faith. It needs help to come to itself and not to flutter around like some shy birds that have fallen out of their nest because they've only half-learned to fly. Faith as a virtue is God's "Yes" to himself in human freedom—I preached that at one time. That's how it is now—exactly that. Pray and hope and believe with me that the Lord soon brings us poor Peters to the other side and once again sets us down on solid ground. But we no longer want to regard him quite as firmly as we sometimes did.

I wanted to write something that hangs together. But reading material and everything else is so happenstance. Even that is a blessing, though. For the first ten weeks I had absolutely nothing. And then with these tied hands nothing much can be done in the way of writing. The few moments when they're free, they're incapable of doing anything. And it's dangerous to make pictures on the table with tied hands! But indeed the angel is here, and the Madonna. And God is in all things. . . .

And now, God bless you. All the best. Greetings to my friends. I'm really counting on you. Good-bye and God protect you.

Georg

To Marianne Hapig and Marianne Pünder, November 22, 1944

Good people,

For once I really have to try and get a word of thanks to you as well. Since the moment of decision is coming closer—as things currently stand, December 7 or 8—I have to expect just about anything. And I do, although I still keep believing in the miracle that stands between me and the gallows. It wasn't for nothing that Urbi's heart suffered for a whole year from the fear of death. She made her offering in connection with what's happening now. The date of her letter, February 15, 1943, is very consoling. And her sacrifice was accepted a few days after something else happened [referring to his visit with Count von Stauffenberg in Bamberg], which is my reason for being here. I have her letter here, with the Sacrament on top of it. . . .

God has taken me at my word and has placed me in the

most extreme position possible. Regardless of anything, I have to say "Yes" a thousand times to him. That's sometimes a great strain on the heart, even from a purely physical point of view. These days, ever since the death of Letterhaus and the others, have been very hard. For myself personally, I see the situation as an intensive education in faith that God is giving me. The whole manner in which everything came about; the determination with which he knocked all the trumps out of my hand and let my self-assurance fall to pieces; the cruel twist in that finally, the statement which is most likely to lead to disaster is in fact wrong: all of this indicates that I must answer a specific question God is asking. It's a tough answer, because on the one hand it must be free with regard to the outcome of the situation, and at the same time it has to be given in hope.

I'm trying hard and discovering ever new sides to God; the world is full of God; God comes even in misery and there is encounter, the need for discernment, and also comfort and blessing. You've already given me so much help. The experience that a piece of bread can be a great grace is a new one for me. But above all, the realization that there are people nearby who care for me and are mindful of me is often a great consolation. And how often you have come right during the hours of depression. I'll never forget the first time, on August 14. I'd just asked Urbi if she could give me a sign. I was coming back right then from a terrible beating, smashed up, hopeless and helpless—and just then, totally unexpectedly, your good things came. The things in themselves are good news, but even more so is that the things bring news of people who break into my isolation.

Since the Sanctissimum [Blessed Sacrament] has been here, the world has become more pleasant again, and so I want to abandon myself to God's freedom and God's goodness and take pains not to refuse him in any way. And yet remain confident that he will bring us across the sea without allowing us to drown.

Thanks again for everything, and I'll see you again, one place or the other. And don't forget to pray and hope with me. All of it, however, is to be consecrated and blessed seed. The hours I've gone through up to now have been rich and, in the mystery of God, have been his will.

Your loyal and grateful
    Max

Late in November, Delp had begun writing down meditations, based on the "gray prayer book" Jesuits were given during their novitiate and containing prayers and devotions, among them the Litany of the Heart of Jesus. He completed only five of these reflections. Then he turned his attention to the season of Advent, which had just begun, writing a series of meditations.

Advent is a time for rousing. Humanity is shaken to the very depths, so that we may wake up to the truth of ourselves. The primary condition for a fruitful and rewarding Advent is renunciation, surrender. Humans must let go of all their mistaken dreams, their conceited poses and arrogant gestures, all the pretenses with which they hope to deceive themselves and others. If they fail to do this stark reality may take hold of them and rouse them forcibly in a way that will entail both anxiety and suffering.

The kind of awakening that literally shocks a person's whole being is part and parcel of the Advent idea. A deep emotional experience like this is necessary to kindle the inner light which confirms the blessing and the promise of the Lord. A shattering awakening; that is the necessary preliminary. Life only begins when the whole framework is shaken. There can be no proper preparation without this. It is precisely in the shock of rousing while he is still deep in the helpless, semi-conscious state, in the pitiable weakness of that borderland between sleep and waking, that a person finds the golden thread which binds earth to heaven and gives the benighted soul some inkling of the fullness it is capable of realizing and is called upon to realize. . . .

The herald angel. Never have I entered an Advent so vitally and intensely alert as I am now. When I pace my cell, up and down, three paces one way and three the other, my hands manacled, an unknown fate in front of me, then the tidings of our Lord's coming to redeem the world and deliver it have quite a different and much more vivid meaning. And my mind keeps going back to the angel someone gave me as a present during Advent two or three years ago. It bore the inscription: "Be of good cheer. The Lord is near." A bomb destroyed it. The same bomb killed the donor and I often have the feeling that he is rendering me some heavenly aid. It would be impossible to endure the horror of these times—like the horror of life itself, could we only see it clearly enough—if there were not this other knowledge which constantly buoys us up and gives us strength: the knowledge of the promises that have been given and fulfilled. And the awareness of the angels of good tidings, uttering their blessed messages in the midst of all this trouble and sowing the seed of blessing where it will sprout in the middle of the night. The angels of Advent are not the bright jubilant beings who trumpet the tidings of fulfillment to a waiting world. Quiet and unseen they enter our shabby rooms and our hearts as they did of old. In the silence of the night they pose God's questions and proclaim the wonders of him with whom all things are possible.

Advent, even when things are going wrong, is a period from which a message can be drawn. May the time never come when men and women forget about the good tidings and promises, when, so immured within the four walls of their prison that their very eyes are dimmed, they see nothing but grey days through barred windows placed too high to see out of. May the time never come when humankind no longer hears the soft footsteps of the herald angel, or his cheering words that penetrate the soul. Should such a time come all will be lost. Then indeed we shall be living in bankruptcy and hope will die in our hearts. For the first thing we must do if we want to raise ourselves out of this sterile life is to open our hearts to the golden seed which God's angels are waiting to sow. And one other thing; we must ourselves throughout these gray days go forth as a bringer of glad tidings. There is so much despair that cries out for comfort; there is so much faint courage that needs to be reinforced; there is so much perplexity that yearns for reasons and meanings. God's messengers, who have themselves reaped the fruits of divine seeds sown even in the darkest hours, know how to wait for the fullness of harvest. Patience and faith are needed, not because we believe in the earth, or in our stars, or our temperament or our good disposition, but because we have received the message of God's herald angel and have ourselves encountered him.

First Sunday in Advent

Unless we have been shocked to our depths at ourselves and the things we are capable of, as well as at the failings of humanity as a whole, we cannot possibly understand the full import of Advent.

If the whole message of the coming of God, of the day of salvation, of approaching redemption, is to seem more than a divinely inspired legend or a bit of poetic fiction two things must be accepted unreservedly.

First, that life is both powerless and futile in so far as by itself it has neither purpose nor fulfillment. It is powerless and futile within its own range of existence and also as a consequence of sin. To this must be added the rider that life clearly demands both purpose and fulfillment.

Secondly it must be recognized that it is God's alliance with humanity, his being on our side, ranging himself with us, that corrects this state of meaningless futility. It is necessary to be conscious of God's decision to enlarge the boundaries of his own supreme existence by condescending to share ours for the overcoming of sin.

It follows that life, fundamentally, is a continuous Advent; hunger and thirst and awareness of lack involve movement toward fulfillment. But this also means that in this progress toward fulfillment humanity is vulnerable; we are perpetually moving toward, and are capable of receiving, the ultimate revelation with all the pain inseparable from that achievement.

On December 8, Delp was unexpectedly visited by his friend, the Jesuit Franz von Tattenbach, who had been authorized by the Jesuit provincial, Franz Xaver Müller (who had replaced Augustin Rösch), to receive Delp's final vows—the vows that had been postponed since August 15. Delp signed the document under the suspicious eyes of the guard and spoke the words of the vow in Latin, punctuated by sobs. The next day he sent a letter to von Tattenbach.

Dear T,

Thanks so much, thank you, thank you. I'm sorry I got so emotional. It was so much at one time. And such an answer to prayer! All during the novena leading up to the 8th, I prayed for a message of mercy. And there it was. *Calculo mundasti ingnito* [You have cleansed with a burning stone]. I hope that my lips were pure and my desire sincere and honest. I have handed over my life completely. The external chains mean nothing anymore, now that God has found me worthy of the *vincula amoris* [chains of love]. A shadow was cast when it seemed that God didn't want me to make my vows on August 15. He was only letting me prepare further. . . .

PS. The rest of the day went very well. A little past noon I got hold of myself again. Do pray for me. I'm astonished and embarrassed that I was so emotional. That's the first time I let myself go like that. I'll have to be careful.

Mass in the evening was full of graces. Please pray the Introit in the same heartfelt spirit I had yesterday! And then, keeping in mind my situation, yesterday's evening prayer. I didn't sleep much last night. For a long time I sat before my tabernacle and just kept praying the Suscipe. In all the variations that applied to me in this situation. Now and then during the late evening I read from the seventh book of the *Republic*: Plato's famous cave image. . . from shadows to reality.

I'd like the formula subscripta [the vow document] kept safe from bombs. It would be too bad for all concerned if it got lost. I was supposed to write a letter saying I was leaving the Society of Jesus. This would be a great substitute.

Many thanks to all and best wishes. You're a good friend, Tatt. It's very good not just to know that, but to have heard and seen it. I've dealt with this whole tough situation so well since then. May God protect you.

Yours, A.

With the taking of his final vows, Delp commenced to write a series of essays on the themes so dear to him: the "godless" state of Western society and a church that stood in need of reform. The discourses were begun during the middle of December.

To M, December 29, 1944

Every now and then someone comes along and tries to impose his own plan on the rest of the world, either because he knows he has stumbled on a universal need or because he thinks he has and overestimates his own infallibility. Such people will never lack followers since so many people long for a well-founded communal home to which they can feel they "belong." Time after time in the end they come to realize that the shelter offered is not all it purports to be—it cannot keep out the wind and the weather. And time and time again the deluded seekers conclude they have been taken in by a mountebank; the man probably had no intention of deliberately deceiving but he was nevertheless a charlatan misleading himself and others.

December 31, 1944

It is difficult to sum up the year now ending in a few words. So much has happened during this last year and yet I cannot see what its real message is for me, or its real achievement. Generally speaking it has not produced anything really effective. Hardship and hunger and violence have intensified and are all now more shattering than anyone could have imagined. The world lies in ruins round us. It is full of hatred and enmity. Everyone clings to their few miserable possessions because these are the last remaining things that they can really call their own.

Spiritually we seem to be in an enormous vacuum. Humanly speaking there is the same burning question—what is the point of it all? And in the end even that question sticks in one's throat. Scarcely anyone can see, or even guess at, the connection between the corpse-strewn battlefields, the heaps of rubble we live in and the collapse of the spiritual cosmos of our views and principles, the tattered residue of our moral and religious convictions as revealed by our behavior. . . .

Finally there are the Vatican and the Church to be considered. So far as concrete and visible influence goes the attitude of the Vatican is not what it was. It is not merely that it seems so because we get no information. Of course it will be shown eventually that the Pope did his duty and more, that he offered peace, that he explored all possibilities to bring about peace negotiations, that he proclaimed the spiritual conditions on which a just peace could be based, that he dispensed alms and was tireless in his work on behalf of the prisoners of war, displaced persons, tracing missing relatives and so on—all this we know and posterity will have documentary evidence in plenty to show the full extent of the papal effort. But to a large extent all this good work may be taken for granted and also to a large extent it leads nowhere and has no real hope of achieving anything. That is the real root of the trouble—among all the protagonists in the tragic drama of the modern world there is not one who fundamentally cares in the least what the Church says or does. We overrated the Church's political machine and let it run on long after its essential driving power had ceased to function. . . .

The Church faces the same tasks that nations and states and the western world in general have to face—the problem of human beings, how they are to be housed and fed and how they can be employed in order to support themselves. In other words we need social and economic regeneration. These are problems for the world, for individual states and nations, and they are also problems for the Church—far more so, for instance, than the question of liturgical forms. If these problems are solved without us, or to our disadvantage, then the whole of Europe will be lost to the Church, even if every altar faces the people and Gregorian chant is the rule in every parish. The supernatural demands a certain amount of expert action in regard to daily life, a degree of natural capacity for living without which life cannot survive. And the Church as an institution, an authority, requires a minimum of religious practice. Otherwise it can only have an individualistic value.

Therefore this year now ending leaves behind it a rich legacy of tasks and we must seriously consider how to tackle them. Above all else one thing is necessary—religious minded people must become more devout; their dedication must be extended and intensified.

And that brings me to my own affairs. Have I grown in stature in the past year? Have I increased my value to the community? How do things stand with me? . . .

An honest examination of conscience reveals much vanity, arrogance and self-esteem; and in the past also a certain amount of dishonesty. That was brought home to me when they called me a liar while I was being beaten up. They accused me of lying when they found I mentioned no name except those I knew they knew already. I prayed hard, asking God why he permitted me to be so brutally handled and then I saw that there was in my nature a tendency to pretend and deceive.

On this altar much has been consumed by fire and much has been melted and become pliable. It has been one of God's blessings, and one of the signs of his indwelling grace, that I have been so wonderfully helped in keeping my vows. He will, I am confident, extend his blessing to my outward existence as soon as I am ready for the next task with which he wishes to entrust me. From this outward activity and intensified inner light new passion will be born to give witness for the living God, for I have truly learned to know him in these days of trial and to feel his healing presence. God alone suffices is literally and absolutely true. And I must have a passionate belief in my mission to humankind, showing the way to a fuller life and encouraging the willing capacity for it. These things I will do wholeheartedly—in opine Domine.

On January 9, Delp, along with Moltke and others of the Kreisau Circle, were led to trial and the death sentence was pronounced. Between January 10 and 11, Delp wrote his farewell letters to Franz von Tattenbach, who was staying in Berlin to be near his friend, Luise Oestreicher, his mother, the Mariannes, and his Jesuit community in Munich.

Dear Luise,

This now has to be a farewell letter. God seems to want me to make the full sacrifice and to take the other road. They've asked for the death sentence, and the atmosphere is so full of hate and hostility that I can't see any other way. The whole trial was driven by hate and hostility. When it came to the points of actual incrimination, the charge fell. But from the first word I knew that the verdict was already decided. Right now my interior position is rather strange. Although I know that if things follow their normal course I'm going to die tonight, I'm not feeling bad at all. Perhaps God is being gracious and sparing me the fear of death up to the end. Or am I supposed to keep on believing that a miracle is going to happen? Adoro and Suscipe [worship and surrender] were the last words of the Epiphany reflection I wrote for you. Let's leave ourselves there. Don't be sad. . . . Pray for me and I'm going to help you as well, you'll see. Now I have to let go completely. Thanks for all your love and kindness and loyalty. And don't hold my moods and immaturity and harshness and nastiness against me.

Greetings to my friends. Whatever happens, it's being offered as seed planted in the earth, and as a blessing and sacrifice. God bless you. Now you're going to have two brothers as guardian angels.

In the enclosed envelope are bits of newspaper, etc. During my loneliest hours I tore these off from what I had for toilet paper so that I could write some words of reflection. I wanted to attach them to a sheet and write something further, and then give them to you as a gift.

May God protect you. Keep up your courage. Thank you and good-bye.

Alfred

To his mother, Maria Delp, January 11, 1945

Dear Mother,

I now have to write you the hardest letter that a child has ever had to write to his mother. It's all become so hopeless that I have to presume I'll be sentenced to death and then executed. Keep your courage up, dear Mother. It's God who decides our fate. We want to give ourselves to him without being spiteful. It's hard on you, dear Mother, but it has to be endured.

Thank you so much for all your love and kindness. You've had such loving concern for us and have done and suffered so much for us. Thank you from the bottom of my heart for every single thing that you've given me and that you've been for me.

Best greetings to Father. I don't think I'll write directly to him. He'll have to be gradually prepared. Just tell him thank-you from me for everything, from the bottom of my heart.

Keep up your courage, dear Mother. Pray for me. When I'm with God, I'll pray and plead on your behalf and make up for all the love I've withheld.

We'll see each other again. After a little while we'll be together again. And then it will be forever and filled with God's joy.

God protect you, Mutterl. Take care that Marianne grows up in the right way. I'll also keep an eye on her. All the best to you.

Your grateful Alfred

To his Jesuit community in Munich, January 11, 1945

Dear Brothers,

Here I am at the parting of the ways and I must take the

other road after all. The death sentence has been passed and the atmosphere is so charged with enmity and hatred that no appeal has any hope of succeeding.

I thank the Society and my brothers for all their goodness and loyalty and help, especially during these last weeks. I ask pardon for much that was untrue and unjust; and I beg that a little help and care may be given to my aged, sick parents.

The actual reason for my condemnation was that I happened to be, and chose to remain, a Jesuit. There was nothing to show that I had any connection with the attempt on Hitler's life, so I was acquitted of that count. . . . The rest of the accusations were far less serious and more factual. There was one underlying theme—a Jesuit is a priori an enemy and betrayer of the Reich. Moltke was treated abominably as well because he was associated with us, especially with Rösch. So the whole proceedings turned into a sort of comedy developing a theme. It was not justice—it was simply the carrying out of the determination to destroy.

May God protect you all. I ask for your prayers. And I will do my best to catch up, on the other side, with all that I have left undone here on earth.

Toward noon I will celebrate Mass once more and then in God's name take the road under his providence and guidance.

In God's blessing and protection,

Your grateful Alfred Delp, S.J.

On January 11, the same day that the death sentence was pronounced, Augustin Rösch was found hiding on a farm near Munich and arrested by the Gestapo. Moltke and the others were executed shortly after the trial, while Delp was left alive, possibly because the Gestapo hoped to gain valuable information from cross-interrogating both him and Rösch. After weeks of agonizing wait, Delp was taken to Plötzensee prison in Berlin on January 31 and executed by hanging on February 2, 1945.

Rösch was freed from the Berlin prison early in May with the liberation of the city and the end of the war.

SOURCES

Delp, Alfred. 2003. *With Bound Hands: A Jesuit in Nazi Germany. The Life and Selected Prison Letters of Alfred Delp*. Edited by Mary Frances Coady. Chicago: Loyola Press.

Sophie Scholl
(1921-43)

*Student and Member
of the "White Rose"*

After years of delay, she could finally begin her studies of science and philosophy at the University of Munich. Within weeks, the twenty-one-year-old and her brother, a student of medicine, were actively trying to expose the tyranny of the Third Reich. Flyers were typed and painstakingly mimeographed, then distributed throughout Munich and other German cities. The flyers denounced Hitler, the war, the cruel treatment of Germans and prisoners of war, the mass murder of Jews. The first flyer appeared in June 1942. The sixth flyer appeared the following February and was placed by the siblings on the university's steps, windowsills, and ledges, with the remainder being thrown from a balcony into the entrance court. The building superintendent at whose feet one of the leaflets had landed took the students to the university's rector, a member of the secret police. Within four days of their arrest, the sentence was carried out. On February 22, both brother and sister were beheaded. Meanwhile, the flyers had reached the allied troops, whose airplanes were dropping them on German cities by the thousands.

Born on May 9, 1921, in Forchtenberg, Sophie Scholl was the second youngest of five children. She was raised in a Protestant home where the Bible was read, and questions of social justice and pacifism were regularly discussed. Her father served as mayor of the town. Her mother was, prior to marriage, a deaconess, a member of a Protestant community of single women who were committed to serving Christ among the sick and poor; during the war years, she had been a nurse to the wounded. After her father lost his post as mayor in 1930, the family moved to Ludwigsburg and in 1932 to Ulm. The family lived in the city center, where her father ran an accounting firm. Sophie attended a girls' school to prepare for college. Her interests ranged from playing the piano and singing to reading, writing short stories, and painting and drawing. When Hitler came to power in 1933, her brother Hans, three years her senior, had organized a youth group as an alternative to the nationalistic Hitler Youth. In 1937, Sophie, her sister Inge, and two of her brothers, Werner and Hans, were arrested by the Gestapo. Sophie spent one day in jail, while her sister and brother Werner were jailed and interrogated for eight days, and the oldest brother, Hans, for five weeks. All were released, but the shock of the arrest completed the family's break with Nazism. Sophie began reading the Bible, the Psalms, St. Augustine, the novels of Thomas Mann, the poetry of Rainer Maria Rilke, Bernanos's Diary of a Country Priest, *and works in philosophy. The family's friendship with leading painters and sculptors allowed her to visit in the summers of 1938 and 1939 the artist colony Worpswede, near Bremen. There she met resident artists, among them Clara Westhoff, the widow of the poet Rainer Maria Rilke, and she saw the works of those who had already been forced to leave Germany.*

Increasingly, Sophie Scholl became concerned about the future of Germany and the threat of the Nazi regime to human freedom. Three school friends, who had been drafted for the war, had already been killed. When her boyfriend, Fritz Hartnagel (1917-2001), entered a military career in the air force, she tried repeatedly to dissuade him from his involvement in war. Her concerns were not lost on Hartnagel: "You create in me a great inner conflict when you ask me about the meaning of all this bloodshed."

After graduating in 1940, Sophie's studies were delayed for two years. Women had been ordered to do community service in the Third Reich. Sophie chose training as a kindergarten teacher at the Fröbel Institute, followed by a practicum at Bad Dürrheim in the Black Forest. When Hitler invaded the Soviet Union, soldiers were drafted for the Russian front, including Fritz Hartnagel, and all prospective college students were ordered to complete an additional six months of "war service." In April 1941, Sophie went to a children's home at the Krauchenwies Camp, near Sigmaringen. But the regime had extended the "war service," so she took another position at a kindergarten, this time in Blumberg, near the Swiss border. Meanwhile, Hartnagel had become a sergeant in the air force and was transferred from Russia to Weimar.

Finally, Sophie arrived in Munich in May 1942 to begin her studies. Shortly thereafter, she joined her brother, Hans, in his resistance work. Hans had already published the first anonymous flyer and come up with a name for their resistance, "The White Rose." The color white reminded him of a white sheet of paper because "a blank page does not yet contain a lie." Other members of the group were the students Alexander Schmorell, Christoph Probst, and Willi Graf. Kurt Huber (1893-1943), a popular philosophy professor at the university, joined the group in early January 1943. A few students, professors, medical doctors, writers, and book dealers had loose contact with members of the White Rose, among them Professor Carl Muth, the Catholic founding editor of the leading Catholic magazine Hochland. A small branch of the White Rose had also sprung up in Hamburg, and contacts were being made to the resistance group "Red Chapel" in Chemnitz and Berlin.

The goal of the White Rose was to encourage passive resistance to the Nazi regime by unmasking its evil. "Every word that comes out of Hitler's mouth is a lie," the fourth leaflet said. "When he says peace, he means war, and when he blasphemously uses the name of the Almighty, he means the power of evil, the fallen angel, Satan. His mouth is the foul-smelling maw of Hell, and his might is at bottom accursed." The leaflet closed with a warning: "We will not be silent. We are your bad conscience. The White Rose will not leave you in peace!"

Writing and distributing flyers seemed an ideal means of passive resistance. The idea had been born one day when a letter without return address had arrived at the Scholl home in Ulm containing a mimeographed sermon by the Catholic bishop of Münster, Clement August Count von Galen. The bishop had been a critic of the Nazis as early as 1934. Many of von Galen's sermons were secretly circulated throughout the country. In them he denounced the Nazis for their racial policies and encouraged the population to withstand the Nazi terror. When, in the summer of 1941, the Nazis' measures of "purifying" the race had expanded from Jews, gypsies, and homosexuals to include the mentally ill, the physically handicapped, the incurably ill, and the aged, von Galen again vented from the pulpit. It was one of these sermons opposing the euthanasia measures that had landed in the family Scholl's mailbox while Hans was home. "Finally someone has the courage to speak," he said to his family about von Galen, "and all you need is a duplication machine."

Members of the group began sending anonymous flyers by mail to those they suspected of a favorable response. Recipients were asked to make copies for further distribution. To divert attention away from Munich, members took the train to Augsburg, Frankfurt, Stuttgart, Freiburg, Saarbrücken, Karlsruhe, and Cologne to post the letters from there. Flyers were also sent from Berlin, Hamburg, Vienna, and Salzburg. The first four flyers were mailed and distributed between June and July 1942. The group's activities came to a halt when Hans Scholl, Alexander Schmorell, and Willi Graf were drafted for military service in Russia. They left Munich by train on July 23, 1942. Sophie went back to Ulm, where her father had been arrested for calling Hitler "a great scourge" a year earlier. The remark had been reported by one of Scholl's office workers. On charges of "defamation" (Heimtücke) Scholl received four months in prison. At night, Sophie stood near the prison with her flute, playing the song "The Thoughts Are Free" for her father. In addition, she was commandeered to an arms factory to work alongside Russian prisoners of war. With the return of Hans and his friends from the Russian front in November of 1943, the group's work resumed. Donors contributed stamps and money for the next round of mailings. Plans were made for a network of student resistance groups in university cities throughout the country. A personal meeting with Dietrich Bonhoeffer had been scheduled for February 25, 1943.

During the 470th anniversary celebration of the University of Munich on January 13, 1943, a speech by a Nazi official had sparked fierce student protests. The official had told women to go home, instead of occupying university slots; they should procreate and bear children for the Führer, he said, and, if necessary, a male Nazi representative would "help out." Sophie hoped the protests would spark a mass uprising. Shortly thereafter, Kurt Huber joined their group. In early February, the German troops were defeated at Stalingrad, exposing the war's senseless human massacre. At night, Hans Scholl and

Alexander Schmorell had painted in black letters on walls and above the entrance of the university the slogans "Liberty," "Down with Hitler," and "Hitler the Mass Murderer." The group's members were confident that the German defeat in Russia and the official's speech would finally open eyes. A sixth flyer was prepared, and 3,000 copies were printed and distributed. After placing flyers in bundles throughout the university, Sophie Scholl dropped the remaining leaflets from a third-story balcony into the atrium below. The superintendent apprehended the two students, the Gestapo was informed, and the names of the other members of the White Rose were discovered. On February 22, 1943, only four days after their arrest, Sophie and Hans Scholl were executed, along with their friend and collaborator Christoph Probst. Sophie Scholl was the first of the three to go to the guillotine. The prison warden observed that "she went without flinching. None of us could believe how this was possible. The executioner said he had never seen anyone die like that." The remaining three White Rose members were tried and condemned to death on April 19, 1943. Alexander Schmorell and Kurt Huber were executed on July 13, and Willi Graf on October 12, 1943.

In a BBC radio speech to German listeners broadcast on June 27, 1943, from exile in the United States, the author Thomas Mann praised the members of the White Rose: "Good, splendid young people! You shall not have died in vain; you shall not be forgotten. The Nazis have raised monuments in Germany to dirty rogues and mean killers—but the German revolution, the real revolution, will tear them down and in their place will memorialize these people, who, at the time when Germany and Europe were still enveloped in the dark of the night, knew and publicly declared: 'A new faith in freedom and honor is dawning'."

In the city of Ulm, a square has been named in honor of

Hans and Sophie Scholl, and since 1972 the school that Sophie attended for eight years (1932-40) has been named the Hans-and-Sophie Scholl Gymnasium.

* * *

To Fritz Hartnagel, Ulm, May 29, 1940

My dear Fritz,

We're having some really glorious early summer weather. If I had the time, I'd stretch out beside the Iller, swim, laze, and try to think of nothing but the beauty around me. It isn't easy to banish all thoughts of the war. Although I don't know much about politics and have no ambition to do so, I do have some idea of right and wrong, because that has nothing to do with politics and nationality. And I could weep at how mean people are, in high-level politics as well, and how they betray their fellow creatures, perhaps for the sake of personal advantage. Isn't it enough to make a person lose heart sometimes? Often my one desire is to live on a Robinson Crusoe island. I'm sometimes tempted to regard mankind as a terrestrial skin disease. But only sometimes, when I'm very tired, and people who are worse than beasts loom large in my mind's eye. But all that matters fundamentally is whether we come through, whether we manage to hold our own among the majority, whose sole concern is self-interest—those who approve of any means to their own ends. It's so overwhelming, that majority, you have to be bad to survive at all. Only one person has ever managed to go straight to God, probably, but who still looks for him nowadays?

Dear Fritz, this whole letter will probably strike you as odd in the extreme. I expect you've so much to see and do that you never have time to think about yourself anymore. That scares me a little.

To Fritz Hartnagel, Ulm, June 22, 1940

How long is it since I wrote to you? Meantime, another of your letters has turned up. However much I always enjoy answering your latest letter, I find it very difficult because it's hard to say things in writing that can only be resolved by conversational toing and froing. I'm perfectly prepared to believe that you simply argue with me for argument's sake when we get onto ideological and political subjects—the two go hand in hand. It's enjoyable, I appreciate that. Personally, though, I've never argued for argument's sake, as you may secretly believe. On the contrary, I've always unconsciously made certain allowances for the profession you're tied to, in the hope that you'll weigh these things more carefully and perhaps make concessions here and there.

I can't imagine two people living together when they differ on these questions in their views, or at least in their activities.

People shouldn't be ambivalent themselves just because everything else is, yet one constantly meets the view that, because we've been born into a world of contradictions, we must defer to it. Oddly enough, this thoroughly un-Christian attitude is especially common among self-styled Christians.

If it were so, how could one expect fate to make a just cause prevail when so few people unwaveringly sacrifice themselves for a just cause?

I'm reminded of an Old Testament story that tells how Moses raised his arms in prayer every hour of the day and night, asking God for victory. As soon as he let them drop, his people forfeited divine favor in battle.

Do people still exist today who never tire of undividedly focusing all their thoughts and desires on a single objective?

That doesn't mean I would range myself on the side of those who are single-hearted in the true sense. Scarcely an hour passes without one of my thoughts flying off at a tangent, and very few of my actions correspond to what I consider right. I'm so often scared of those actions, which loom over me like dark mountains, that all I want to do is cease to exist, or become a grain of earth, or a fragment of bark. But this often overpowering desire is equally bad because it only stems from weariness.

Weariness is my principal possession. It keeps me silent when I ought to speak out—when I ought to admit to you what concerns us both. I put it off till later. How I wish I could live awhile on an island where I could do and say what I want, instead of having to be patient indefinitely.

To Fritz Hartnagel, Ulm, June 28, 1940

Hans writes that he's busy day and night. He's quite fit again (so he says) and working at a field hospital—near Rheims, I think. He'd been helping to nurse the wounded from Soissons. Most people here take the attitude: Who cares how the war turns out as long as my son or husband soon comes home in one piece?

It looks as if the French were only interested in their home comforts. I'd have been more impressed if they'd defended Paris to the last round, regardless of all the art treasures housed there, even if they'd achieved nothing, or nothing of any immediate value. But expediency is everything these days, and true purpose no longer exists. Nor does honor, I suppose. Saving your own skin is the main thing.—Well, now that France is in the Führer's hands, will home leave cease to be so out of the question?

If I didn't know I'll probably outlive many of my elders, I'd sometimes shudder at the spirit that governs history today. Now that the mighty lion has killed, the jackal and the hyena are venturing forth to claim their share.

I'm sure your attitude to all that's happening today is quite unlike mine. You have plenty to do. I'm doing work that's the same in wartime as in peacetime. Sometimes I do it gladly, often I don't. I'm sure you find it unfeminine, the way I write to you. It must seem absurd for a girl to worry her head about politics. She's supposed to let her feminine emotions rule her thoughts. But I find that thoughts take precedence, and that emotions often lead you astray because you can't see big things for the little things that may concern you more directly—personally, perhaps. It's the same with children. You can't provide them with all they need to console them when they cry, not right away, because it's often better for their development if you don't give in to your immediate feelings.

To Fritz Hartnagel, Ulm, July 19, 1940

My dear Fritz,
Just a quick line before going to sleep. I can't write a real letter, I'm too tired. I went for a two-hour cycle ride with Inge [*her sister*] this afternoon. It was lovely, and I came home rich. It's so grand to be able to take things, just like that, without depriving anyone. It's so good that the fields and the forests and clouds never change, unlike us human beings. (We remain the same too, or so it might seem to a giant, but our mutual relationships are constantly changing.) And even when you think that everything's about to end, the moon reappears in the sky the following night, the same as ever. And the birds continue to sing as sweetly and busily without worrying whether there's any point in it. Have you noticed the way they tilt their little heads to the sky and sing with complete abandon, and how their little throats swell? It's good that such things are always with us. You have them too. It's enough to gladden one's heart, isn't it?
Yours, Sofie

To Fritz Hartnagel, Bad Dürrheim, August 19, 1940

I got a letter from you this morning. I'm always waiting eagerly for letters at present. Very many thanks.—Because I'm on afternoon rest duty (i.e. have to make sure that none of the twenty children who've been sleeping on the terrace for two hours speaks or does anything else), I can reply right away.

I sometimes think of last summer too, but I don't brood about it. I don't have the time.

I think you misunderstand my views on your profession. Or rather, I think that the soldier's profession today is different from what you described. A soldier has to swear an oath, after all, so his job is to carry out his government's orders. Tomorrow he may have to comply with a view diametrically opposed to yesterday's. His profession is obedience. So the soldierly attitude isn't really a profession. In your ideal conception of it, it really accords with the moral demands made on every individual. I can well appreciate that you regard your profession as an educative one, but I think that's only a part of it. How can a soldier have an honest attitude, as you put it, when he's compelled to lie? Or isn't it lying when you have to swear one oath to the government one day and another the next? You have to allow for that situation, and it's already arisen before now. You weren't so much in favor of a war, to the best of my knowledge, yet you spend all your time training people for it.

You surely don't believe it's the job of the armed forces to teach people an honest, modest, sincere attitude. And as for your comparing this to Christianity, I believe a person can be a Christian without belonging to a church. Besides, a Christian isn't compelled to be anything other than what his principal commandments require of him. If a soldier's commandment is to be loyal, sincere, modest, and honest, he certainly can't obey it, because if he receives an order, he has to carry it out, whether he considers it right or wrong. If he doesn't carry it out, he's dismissed, isn't he?

Forgive me if I've been vague or incoherent in what I've written. The little rascals are such a handful. All one can do is scold them the whole time. But most of the pranks they play to make themselves look big are so childishly silly I'm tempted to laugh behind my hand.

To Fritz Hartnagel, Ulm, March 22, 1941

I received some unwelcome news today: I've got to go into the *Arbeitsdienst*. However, I've already come to terms with my immediate future. I always try to acclimatize myself as quickly as possible (mentally, too, and to new ideas). It's an aid to maximum independence from all outward circumstances, pleasant or unpleasant. I've become so expert at self-adjustment that I got over my annoyance at the RAD (*Reichsarbeitsdienst*) in five minutes flat, and when I left school, Fräulein Kretschmer defined my most salient characteristic as imperturbability. Perhaps it'll compensate a little for my moodiness during your leave if I quote two lines from a graduation day poem: "She (S. Scholl) always was a cheerful sort, and nothing ever put her out." I'm rather dumbfounded myself at the impression I make on such people.

Diary entry, Krauchenwies, April 10, 1941

I arrived here four days ago.

I'm sharing a dormitory with ten other girls. I often have to close my ears to their chatter in the evenings. Every time I join in, it seems like a concession, and I regret it. I've managed to stay pretty much in the background so far, thanks to my shyness. I wish I could keep it up, but I'm forever catching myself showing off in little ways. It's awful, my craving for recognition. Even as I write that, I'm wondering how it will look on paper. It's destructive of mental harmony.

At nights, while the others are cracking jokes (I haven't entirely steered clear of those, I'm afraid), I read St. Augustine. I have to read slowly, it's so hard to concentrate, but read I do, even when I don't feel like it. I also read some of Thomas Mann's *Zauberberg* in the lunch break today.

Diary entry, Krauchenwies, April 11, 1941

This evening, as I glanced quickly out of the window of our cheerful, bustling room, I saw the yellow skyline through the bare trees. It suddenly struck me then that it was Good Friday. I was saddened by the strangely remote and detached sky. Or by all the laughing people who were so divorced from the sky. I felt excluded, both from the cheerful company around me and from the indifferent sky.

I would very much like to go to church. Not the Protestant one, where I listen critically to what the parson says, but the other one, where I tolerate everything and have only to be open and receptive. But is that the right one?

I'm afraid I showed off again for a moment this evening. I didn't lie or exaggerate, but it occurred to me while speaking that I was eager to impress.

I'm gradually becoming acclimatized, I'm afraid. I shall take myself in hand. Reading at nights will be a help.

Diary entry, Blumberg, October 11, 1941

I came back yesterday to find a letter and a little book from Professor [*Carl*] Muth [*a distinguished Catholic writer and founder and editor of the Catholic magazine* Hochland] awaiting me. Yesterday I was delighted, but today I can't summon up the energy to be delighted anymore. I'm so tired, I'd like nothing better than to go to bed right now and sleep forever.

Now I'm back at the Schüles' again. I really came so that I could play the organ in the chapel afterward, or simply be in the chapel. I'd so much like to believe in miracles. I'd so much like to believe that I can acquire strength through prayer. I can't achieve anything by myself.

Muth wrote that we must pray for Otl [*Aichinger, a writer, artist, and family friend of the Scholls*]. I'd never thought of praying for him—he never seemed to need it at all. Who doesn't, though? Even a saint does. . . .

I'm so terribly tired, and I'm always prone to such futile, ridiculous mental digressions.

Thou hast created us in Thine image.

I should like, as that Prophet did, to ask God for visible evidence of himself. Or has that ceased to be necessary? I should like to spread myself out like a cloth for him to collect his dew in.

Diary entry, Blumberg, November 4, 1941

I visited the church on Saturday afternoon, ostensibly to play the organ. It was absolutely empty. It's a colorful little chapel. I tried to pray. I kneeled down and tried to pray, but even as I did so I thought: Better hurry, so you can get up before someone comes. I wasn't afraid of strangers seeing me on my knees, but I was afraid Hildegard [*a colleague at the camp*] might walk in, so I couldn't disclose my innermost thoughts. That's probably wrong, probably a false sense of shame. And that's why I hurried through my prayer and got up just the same as I'd kneeled down. I wasn't ready—I was simply trying to rush things. And now I'm generally in such a mundane frame of mind, without the urge. I'm homesick the whole time, that's all.

Diary entry, Blumberg, November 10, 1941

Sometimes I feel I can forge a path to God in an instant, purely by yearning to do so—by yielding up my soul entirely. If I beseech him, if I love him far above all else, if my heart aches so badly because I'm apart from him, he ought to take me unto himself. But that entails many steps, many tiny little steps, and the road is a very long one. One mustn't lose heart. Once, when I'd lost heart because I kept backsliding, I didn't dare pray anymore. I decided not to ask anything more of God until I could enter his presence again. That in itself was a fundamental yearning for God. But I can always ask him, I know that now.

Diary entry, Blumberg, December 12, 1941

I realize that when I love people very much, I can't do better than include them in my prayers. If I love people in all sincerity, I love them for God's sake. What better thing can I do than take that love to God?

God grant that I come to love Fritz, too, in His name.

To Lisa Remppis, Blumberg, December 12, 1941

I still find life so rich and good, in spite of everything, but people fail to make good use of it. Perhaps it would do us good to become really poor, so as to be better prepared for less ephemeral riches. Don't people look for compensation when they're deprived of so much, and don't they then realize that they let themselves be distracted by affluence and set their hearts on unworthy things? Perhaps they first have to discover that they possess a heart.

How fortunate that, even in the army and much as it makes them suffer, there are people who retain their inner independence because they don't rely on things that others can deprive them of, and that we're privileged to number such people among our friends.

Freiburg Cathedral, which I've often visited in recent months, is really beautiful, and it makes me feel warm inside to be there. I'll be there again the day after tomorrow. I'll write and tell you about it.

Sheet from a letter, Munich, June 23, 1942

There's a bird squawking outside in a tree whose golden-green top is lighted by the mellow, slanting rays of the evening sun. I'm reminded of the passage in your nice letter from Russia in which you speak of Nature being "unredeemed." I've always felt, and I still do now, that I can hear the most consummate harmony resounding from field and forest. Last Sunday, as I made my way into a big, peaceful mountain valley bathed in warm evening air that was already obscuring little details and throwing big, clear-cut outlines into relief, all my usual worries seemed to fall away from me like useless leaves, and I began to judge my preoccupations by an entirely different criterion. It seemed to me that man alone had disrupted this wonderful harmony, which I can also detect in a Bach fugue. I felt as if man had set himself apart from this harmony, and that it was lingering on, but without him. That's why I found it inconceivable that Nature should stand in need of redemption. Yesterday evening, or rather, after midnight, while I was walking back with someone through the English Garden . . . , it suddenly occurred to me that Nature might have to be redeemed by death, however innocent the death that animals and plants must die.

Six weeks after arriving in Munich, Sophie discovered that the authors of the anonymous leaflet disseminated throughout Munich and elsewhere had been her brother Hans and his friend

Alexander Schmorell. She then became involved in the White Rose, which distributed the second leaflet during the third week of June. Its authors asked, "Have the Germans 'sunk into a terminal sleep from which there is no awakening, ever, ever again?'" The reply was, "It seems that way . . . if the German does not arouse himself from this lethargy, if he does not protest whenever he can against this gang of criminals, if he doesn't feel compassion for the hundreds of thousands of victims—not only compassion, no, much more: guilt. . . . *Everyone shrugs off this guilt, falling asleep again with his conscience at peace. But he can't shrug it off; everyone is* guilty, guilty, guilty!"

Diary entry, June 29, 1942

My God, I can only address you falteringly. I can only offer you my heart, which is wrested away from you by a thousand desires. Being so weak that I cannot remain facing you of my own free will, I destroy what distracts me from you and force myself to turn to you, for I know that I'm happy with you alone. Oh, how far from you I am, and the best thing about me is the pain I feel on that account. But I'm often so torpid and apathetic. Help me to be singlehearted and remain with me. If I could only once call you Father, but I can hardly address you as "YOU." I do so [as one that speaks] to a great Unknown. I know that you'll accept me if I'm sincere, and that you'll hear me if I cling to you. Teach me to pray. Better to suffer intolerable pain than to vegetate insensibly. Better to be parched with thirst, better to pray for pain, pain, and more pain, than to feel empty, and to feel so without truly feeling at all. That I mean to resist.

Two more leaflets followed and were distributed and mailed out in mid-July. The third leaflet offered concrete examples of passive resistance. "The meaning and goal of passive resistance

*is to topple National Socialism, and in this struggle we must
not recoil from any course, any action, whatever its nature. At
all points we must oppose National Socialism, wherever it is
open to attack. We must soon bring this monster of a state to
an end." The general ways of resistance were listed as follows:
"Sabotage in armament plants and war industries. Sabotage at
all gatherings, rallies, public ceremonies, and organizations of
the Nationalist Party. Obstruction of the smooth functioning
of the war machine. . . . Sabotage in all the areas of science
and scholarship which further the continuation of the war—
whether in universities, technical schools, laboratories, research
institutes, or technical bureaus. Sabotage in all cultural insti-
tutions which could potentially enhance the 'prestige' of the
fascists among the people. Sabotage in all branches of the arts.
. . . Do not give a penny to public drives. . . . Do not contribute
to collections of metal, textiles, and the like. Try to convince all
your acquaintances (including those in the lower social classes)
of the senselessness of continuing, of the hopelessness of this
war; of our intellectual and economic enslavement at the hands
of the National Socialists; of the destruction of all moral and
religious values; and urge them to* passive resistance!*" Sophie
writes in her diary on August 6, 1942:*

I'm so weak-willed that I can't even fulfill and act on my
own perceptions, nor can I ever renounce my personal volition,
which I know to be imprudent and self-seeking, and surrender
myself to His. Yet I'd like to, and I'm happy to reflect that he
is the ruler of all things. Being unable to relinquish my foolish
hold on it voluntarily, I pray every night that he may wrest
my will away and subject me to his—if only I didn't stand in
my own way. I pray for a compassionate heart, for how else
could I love? I who am so shallow in everything must pray
for everything. A child can be compassionate, but I too often

forget the sufferings that ought to overwhelm me, the sufferings of mankind. I place my powerless love in your hands, that it may become powerful.

Diary entry, October 10, 1942

Whenever I pray, the words drain out of me. The only ones I can remember are "Help me!" I can't offer up any other prayer for the simple reason that I'm still far too abject to be able to pray. So I pray to learn how to pray.

This morning I was at the Schmorells', looking for some books in Schurik's room. How often one wishes oneself into a state of self-deception! Months ago I still believed my affection for Schurik was greater than for many others, but how false this illusion was from the start. It was simply my vanity that wanted to possess a person who was worth something in the estimation of others. Oh, how I disgust myself! How ludicrously I distort my own image, and—no, I long for the chance to prove myself in a different way.

How beautiful the sky was today, how wonderful and beautiful the innocent trees and plants, yet the sight of them didn't make me happy; it filled me with gentle melancholy. [They were] an innocent reminder of guilt—my own guilt.

To Fritz Hartnagel, Ulm, October 28, 1942

My dear Fritz,

I received a letter from you today, and I thank you for it with all my heart. I wish I could back you up with what I know and am in the arguments you're so often compelled to have with your brother officers. The fact that their whole inner being doesn't rebel at that law of nature, the conquest of the weak by the strong, strikes me as dreadful and degenerate, or utterly and completely insensitive. Even a child is filled with horror when forced to witness the defeat and destruction of a weak animal by a strong one. I was always deeply moved and saddened by that inescapable fact, not only as a child but later on as well, and I racked my brains for some way of remaining aloof from this universal state of affairs. The sight of an innocent little mouse in a trap always brought tears to my eyes, and I can only attribute my regained and continuing happiness to forgetfulness, which is no solution. Nor *can* there be any solution here on earth. It says in Romans: "For the earnest expectation of the creature waiteth for the manifestation of the sons of God. For the creature was made subject to vanity, *not* willingly, but by reason of him who hath subjected the same in hope." Fritz, you simply must read that chapter yourself, either when you've finished this letter or right away. And read the wonderful words at the beginning: "For the law of the Spirit of life in Christ Jesus hath made me free from the law of sin and death." Aren't they terribly, terribly poor, the people who neither know nor believe that? Their poverty ought to make us eternally patient with them (that, and the knowledge of our own weakness, for what would we amount to by ourselves?), even if their stupid arrogance tends to infuriate us. If they believe that might must prevail, ask them if they think that man and beast should be placed entirely on a par, or that man additionally shares in a world of the spirit. Ask them—they're bound, in their arrogance, to endorse the latter. And then ask them if it isn't ignominious for the flesh and brute force to triumph in the world of the spirit, if other laws don't prevail in that world than in the world of the flesh, if an ailing inventor or—to get away from the dubious realm of technology—an ailing poet or philosopher doesn't count for more and command more strength in the world of the spirit than a brainless athlete—a Hölderlin [*meaning the poet*

Friedrich Hölderlin] more than a Schmeling [*in reference to the German boxer Max Schmeling*] (may Hölderlin pardon the juxtaposition, which pains me too). Yes, we do believe in the victory of the stronger, but the stronger is the spirit. And the fact that this victory may perhaps come to pass in a world other than our own limited one (beautiful though it is, it's nonetheless small)—no, it already does so here, but only as a radiant prospect visible to all—makes it no less worthy of attainment.

When they say that Nature is good because it was created by God, they forget that man, and the whole of Nature with him, fell after the creation, which God had described as "very good." How meekly they submit to God's judgment all of a sudden! I've never, ever believed that anyone thinks it good for a weak country to be attacked by a powerful army. Even the worst of men, however pleased he may be in other respects, won't regard that as a good thing. The supremacy of brute force always implies that the spirit has been destroyed or at least banished from view. Is that what they want, the people who argue with you? Oh, those lazy thinkers with their sloppy notions of life and death! Only life engenders life, or have they seen a dead woman give birth to a child? Or what about a stone, which can't be denied a semblance of life, since it exists and has a fate of its own—have they ever seen one reproduce itself? They've never reflected on the absurdity of the proposition that only death engenders life, and their urge for self-preservation will lead to their self-destruction. They know nothing of a world of the spirit in which the law of sin and death has been overcome.

Upon the return from Russia of Hans Scholl and his friends in early November, the operation resumed. The fifth and sixth flyers were no longer under the heading of the White Rose but were titled "Leaflets of the Resistance." Willi Graf and Kurt

Huber wrote the fifth leaflet and Kurt Huber the sixth leaflet, which Hans and Sophie Scholl distributed at the university on February 18—the day of their arrest.

Letter to Fritz Hartnagel, Ulm, January 3, 1943

My dear Fritz,

Maybe an airmail letter will have a better chance of reaching you, so I'll use up the blank side after all. I'm following the news with far more interest now that I know where you are. I hope you're all right, and that not even hardship and the din of battle can throw you off course. Hardship tends to blunt the senses, I'm sure, but remember: *Un esprit dûr, du coeur* TENDRE! It often makes me unhappy that I'm not a vehicle for universal suffering. That way I could at least remove part of my guilt from those who are undeservedly having to suffer so much more than I. I'm so much with you in spirit these days that I often feel we're bound to bump into one another, but I keep on worrying and wondering how things are with you. You know the value of a human life, and we have to know what we're risking for it. What a responsibility you bear! However, you do know a source of strength.

And now, God bless you. Yours,
Sophie

Sophie Scholl's last letter was sent from Munich to Lisa Rempss on February 17, 1943.

Dear Lisa,

I've just been playing the Trout Quintet on the phonograph. Listening to the andantino makes me want to be a trout myself. You can't help rejoicing and laughing, however moved or sad at heart you feel, when you see the springtime clouds in the sky and the budding branches sway, stirred by the wind, in the bright young sunlight. I'm so much looking forward to the spring again. In that piece of Schubert's you can positively feel and smell the breezes and scents and hear the birds and the whole of creation cry out for joy. And when the piano repeats the theme like cool, clear, sparkling water—oh, it's sheer enchantment.

Let me hear from you soon. Lots of love,
   Sophie

SOURCES

Dumbach, Annette, and Jud Newborn. 2006. *Sophie Scholl and the White Rose.* Oxford: Oneworld.

Jens, Inge, ed. 1987. *The Heart of the White Rose: Letters and Diaries of Hans and Sophie Scholl.* Trans. J. Maxwell Brownjohn. New York: Harper and Row.

Scholl, Inge. 1983 [1970]. *The White Rose: Munich 1942-1943.* Trans. Arthur R. Schultz. Introduction Dorothee Sölle. Middletown, CT: Wesleyan University Press.

JOCHEN KLEPPER
(1903-42)

Novelist, Poet, Hymnist

Known to Germans for his Christian novels, essays, radio broadcasts, and hymn texts, the author and journalist had recently begun work on a novel on the life of Katharina von Bora, Martin Luther's wife. But his personal life was weighed down by worries: prone to chronic headaches, he suffered from the repercussions of being married to a Jew in Nazi Germany and the fears for his wife's life and that of her two daughters. Jews were being deported to concentration camps in droves, and Aryan spouses of Jews were to file for divorce. In 1939, the older daughter had been safely shipped off to England via Sweden with the help of Quakers. But the younger daughter remained at home. As the Nazi measures against Jews grew, he desperately sought to obtain a travel visa for the younger daughter. When the visa was denied and deportation was imminent, he prepared for the final exit. Friends saw a sign posted by the front door that cautioned of the danger of gas. Inside the home, they found his body and those of his wife and daughter, along with a diary and the order of worship for their Christian funeral.

Jochen Klepper was born on March 22, 1903, in Beuthen an

der Oder, a town of 3,000. He had two older sisters, Margot and Hildegard ("Hilde"), and two younger brothers, Erhard and Wilhelm. His father, the town pastor, hoped that his oldest son would follow in his footsteps. After attending the gymnasium in Glogau, Klepper studied Protestant theology in Breslau. There his professor was the Luther scholar Rudolf Hermann (1887-1962), who would later help edit Luther's collected works (Weimarer Ausgabe). Klepper saw in Hermann a father figure and mentor, and he planned to write his theological thesis on the Lutheran Pietist August Hermann Francke. But when his lucrative journalistic work with the Protestant press association in Breslau took precedence, the theological studies were broken off, his thesis remained unfinished, and the pastorate was discarded, much to the father's chagrin. Klepper, in turn, viewed his studies as foundational to his writing craft. He was among the first in Germany to broadcast Protestant morning devotions. And publishers and the public seemed to appreciate his theological insights woven into his essays, novels, and monographs.

In 1929, Klepper met Johanna Stein, thirteen years his senior. She was a widow with two young daughters, Brigitte and Renate, Jewish, and a descendent of one of Germany's leading families in the apparel industry. Against the father's objections, the couple was married on March 28, 1931, by the justice of the peace. The following year, Klepper and his new family moved to Berlin, where he was hired by Radio Berlin and where the couple built a house. In 1933, Klepper's first novel was published, titled Der Kahn der fröhlichen Leute *("The Canoe of Happy People"), a light-hearted story about life in the area of the upper Oder River of Klepper's childhood, for which the film rights were sold.*

When, in January 1933, Hitler came to power, the mass media were centralized. Klepper lost his job due to his member-

ship, until 1932, in a liberal German political party, the SPD, and partially because his wife was Jewish. For two years, he worked as a copyeditor with the Ullstein publishing house until he was let go there for similar reasons. In 1937, his novel Der Vater *("The Father") appeared featuring as protagonist the Protestant Prussian King Frederick Wilhelm I. Klepper's king regarded himself as the "foremost servant of the state," who sought God's wisdom and guidance for the good of the people. Klepper had worked on the novel for three years, since Hitler's rise to power, and the novel's benevolent and God-fearing Prussian monarch and his court contrasted sharply with Germany's present commander in chief, Hitler, and the fanatical Führer cult of a hate-filled, violent Nazi regime. Within four years, the novel sold 90,000 copies, despite the state's prohibiting booksellers to promote the book. With its implicit critique of the Nazi regime, the book was highly popular not only in Prussia, but also among officers of the army. The novel's success led to Klepper's friendship with the son of Frederick I, King Frederick the Great, and his wife, Hermine, who at the time were living in exile in the Netherlands. But repercussions followed; within months of the novel's publication, Klepper was barred from the Reich's author guild, hence prohibited from publishing. In a letter to Professor Hermann, he quotes the mentor's own words: "Only the Christian can fully live in the present because his past has been canceled and his future is already certain."*

The prohibition to publish was followed by the Nazis' order to tear down the newly built house in the south of Berlin, based on a zoning issue. Property was bought in Berlin-Nikolassee and a new house built. More modest than the previous one, it was again furbished with fine furniture and decorated with fresh flowers and valuable art work. Among the religious pieces in the home was a crucifix of the Reformation era, carved an-

gels and apostles, a near life-size Madonna with child, a statue of the scourged Jesus, and a Gothic wooden statue of Christ extending his hands in a blessing. The couple had purchased the blessing Christ statue while in Augsburg in October 1942.

For Klepper, the home was the place of Christian formation and a metaphor for the eternal home with God. With the tragic loss of the previous home and construction of a new one, his plans for a new novel took on personal meaning. Since 1936, he had conceived of writing Das Ewige Haus *("The Eternal Home"), a book that was to portray the life of Katharina of Bora and her estate, Wachsdorf, Zülsdorf, and the Black Monastery at Wittenberg. Having grown up in a pastor's home, Klepper was intrigued by "the first pastor's home." In 1937, together with his wife, whom he called "Bore," Klepper traveled to Magdeburg, Wittenberg, Erfurt, and Weimar to research Katharina's life through that of Luther's. But progress on the manuscript was slow, and only the first chapter, Katharina's flight from the cloister, exists. In early December 1942, Brigitte and her husband Karl in England shared with him the good news of the birth of their first child; they had named the baby Katharina.*

In 1938, after years of hesitation, Klepper's wife, Johanna ("Hanni"), converted to Christianity and was baptized. The couple had their marriage solemnized in a church wedding. The baptism of the younger daughter, Renate, followed in 1940, while Klepper continued in his efforts to secure her a travel visa. Added to these worries were the Nuremberg Laws, demanding that Aryans divorce their Jewish spouses. Klepper rejected his wife's offer for a divorce. With the growing persecution of the Jews, which Klepper considered a crime against God, arose the question about the role of the church. Like his mentor, Professor Hermann, and his close friend the Catholic novelist and poet Reinhold Schneider (1903-58), Klepper regarded with skepticism the Confessing Church, which had grown out of the 1933 Pastors Emergency League ("Pfarrernotbund") of Protestant pastors and had become, with the 1934 Barmen Declaration, a resistance movement against the Nazis and its centralized national church ("Reichskirche"). Many Protestants in holding fast to Luther's two-kingdom doctrine did not see in the Confessing Church a manifestation of the true Christian faith, but the church's undue intervening into state politics, hence the needless provocation of church conflict. Repeatedly, Klepper was approached by pastors who were members of the Confessing Church to offer his artistic talents in their support; repeatedly, he declined, despite the friendly relations he maintained.

Klepper's stance toward the Confessing Church was motivated less by politics than his understanding of the scriptures and Lutheran piety. Since Hitler's coming to power in 1933, his diary entries were preceded by a scripture passage, allowing him to view the war's horrors in the light of God's word. The biblical passages quoted came largely from the Losungen, *a booklet of randomly selected scriptures with reflections for each day of the year that was—and still is—published annually by the Bruderhof community at Herrnhut. The Bruderhof community of Lutheran Pietists had been founded by one of August Hermann Francke's pupils, Nikolaus Count Ludwig von Zinzendorf, on the estate named Herrnhut, "the Lord's watch." The diary entries were to help Klepper focus in his writing on the cause of Christ. In 1938, Klepper was allowed to publish by special permission his cycle of lyrical poetry, titled* Kyrie. *In 1940, Klepper was drafted into the army serving in Poland, the Balkans, and the Soviet Union between December 1940 and October 1941. To his disappointment, he was discharged early, and dishonorably so, on account of his non-Aryan marriage.*

In November 1942, the younger daughter's visa for Sweden arrived, but Germany denied her a travel visa, meaning her deportation to a concentration camp was imminent. At a personal meeting with the Reich's minister for the interior, Wilhelm Frick, who admired the author, Klepper was told that shortly all marriages between Aryans and Jews would be forcefully dissolved, meaning that his wife, too, would be deported. After instructing his sister, Hildegard, on his last will, he made his final diary entry. On December 10, 1942, after more than a year of intense deliberations, the three members of the Klepper household took sleeping pills, turned on the stove's gas, and committed suicide.

During the war years, Klepper's hymns offered Christians a sense of solace and hope. Today, his hymns are included in Germany's Catholic and Protestant church hymnals. Three hymns are found in the Catholic Gotteslob, *and twelve are included in the* Evangelisches Gesangbuch—*a number only surpassed by the hymns of Martin Luther and Paul Gerhardt.*

* * *

Klepper kept a diary for ten years, starting in April 1932; daily scripture verses were included beginning on December 7, 1933. The diary was kept also while he was in the army, between January 1 and October 8, 1941, though without scripture entries.

I can only say one thing about this boycotting of Jewish businesses: I grieve about the Protestant church [in Germany]. God is distancing himself from us. But I cannot let go of the church, am driven to recognize in it the core of the early church. . . . And also I cannot deny it: I long for preaching. There is nothing that touches me more than the prophets—and Luther is, in my opinion, one of them. I want to be no more than a Protestant poet. It makes any desire for a great breakthrough vanish in me. What is more horrible? To be a people like the Jews who feel God's hand weighing heavily upon them? Or, to be a people like us Germans who have to give an account of this heavy hand? Again and again I am wondering about what horrible future force is being born in some young Jew these days. But in me, too, something is being born that touches upon the core of my life.   —Wednesday, March 29, 1933

The rehearsal [for a broadcast] had to be canceled. No copies of the manuscript had been made because the firm with which the radio station had been collaborating so well up until now is Jewish. The records I had ordered were taken away from me because either the record company or the composer . . . or the conductor is Jewish. My most reliable anchor man I had to send away because he is Jewish. And for the rest, the broadcast station is almost like the Nazi barracks: uniforms, uniforms of Party associations.

The worst to me are the women of the National Socialist Party. They, too, bear the guilt for the political radicalization of the children.

I am not an anti-Semite because no true believer can be one. I am not a philo-Semite because no true believer can be one. But I believe in the mystery of God which he has ordained in Judaism; and that is why I suffer greatly that the church should be permitting the present circumstances. I have an inkling of what it means to be "God's slave."

—Thursday, March 30, 1933

In no way am I regarding daily life as an enemy. Rather, I stick to it: it's the appropriate attitude to have for a Christian and an artist; and the important break will come and the great dividing line between the arts, the Christian faith, and my beloved country. If God were not to exist, everything would be indifferent to me, happiness or misfortune, good or evil, death or life. But if God exists, then and even more so everything is to be indifferent to me; then he can do with me as he pleases. One of my most basic sentiments is gratitude, regardless of how much I suffer from evil and guilt. My nerves are taut, but my soul is still. The circumstances are chaotic, but my future is ordered and secure. —Tuesday, April 3, 1933

I really cannot say that Christianity per se gives me great comfort. Its paradoxes are simply too incisive for that. What, after all, is sanctification, which supposedly bears fruit? I only know one thing: that the direct speech of God to human beings by means of the scriptures, that the mirroring of all things in my life in such speech are what is most important to me. I only know that among the manifold options in life there are only two ordering principles: concentration on the particular book [I'm working on] and the surrender to God's direct speech, which dissolves all visible ordering principles.
—Wednesday, March 13, 1935

From a hymn verse in the *Losungen* of the Bruderhof: "that while suffering I should praise Him, that's what He desires."

I refuse to compare my life to the more difficult life of someone else, thereby deriving comfort. Instead, I grieve about all the wasted, lost, unreachable great possibilities of this serious life here on earth.

And above it all, there is the gloom and heaviness of the political situation. The way things are with Germany, France, Italy, Greece, Russia in their various interconnections and increasing conflicts can only be called, in the words of Eugen Diesel, "the disaster of the nations." And we have sunk into it the deepest. —Friday, March 15, 1935

Great people suffer under their mission. But little people, I sometimes think, suffer even more, namely from the lack of a mission in their life. The fear of having no mission, of seeing life as empty and draining away can be terrifying.

—Friday, September 13, 1935

On reading the newly released Luther book by Rudolph Thiel

I thank God that during these bitter weeks he has again placed Luther into my hands; for his language is the only type of language I can understand and that can move me; it is the only one I understand without any labor or effort. His themes are: fear as the mark of one's election, your will be done on earth as it is in heaven, the right to live out this present life from the Bible's perspective [as] this incomprehensible possibility that unshackles every single day. Not seeing, but trusting divine providence! To insist that the power of sin remains active throughout one's life! To be allowed to break with all reason!

Only one question was not asked in this Luther book, and I am wondering when I will find it in his writings, the one about the "sin that quenches the Holy Spirit"—a question that seems to me inexplicably and disconcertingly connected with that of the Jews. But then the Jews still have God's promises!

Upon remembering a prayer said a few days earlier during a walk alone that his wife might see a sign of God's presence

I prayed that [a sign] might become visible to Hanni, since she is so sober, level-headed, and reticent. During my walk, I was repeatedly overtaken by the thought that God had already given his sign, once and for all, in the cross. But even if one were to put it up somewhere in the home, if one were to put it on one's desk—and not just for art's sake—it might communicate religious fervor only and falsehood.

Around ten o'clock Hanni came back home. Only prior to going to sleep did she tell me that on the way she had "seen something that gave her pause." From afar, she had seen suspended between two trees something dark, and then it became clearer—between the top of two trees—the cross with the crucified one; and as she came closer, it disappeared, though there was no shadow of branches that might have suggested it.

Such things are difficult. Right now and even earlier (though unlike now) I prayed that Hanni might believe, which was "permissible." But to pray for a sign—that is not permissible, though one cannot help but believing that it worked.

—Sunday and Monday, September 22-23, 1935

Open your mouth wide and I will fill it.—Psalm 81:10

To do biblical exegesis by telling the story of a human life, that is what fascinates me! That is what I keep asking from God in all my dismay. It is the reason that I cannot let go of Frederick Wilhelm, because each phase of his life relates to a scripture passage and through the impressions of his life was revealed also the meaning of the biblical word in a way that had never been revealed to me before.

Katharina von Bora: "The Son of Man has no place to put his head."

There are times where all "success" is only temptation; but there can also be times where all success means justification.

—Monday, February 17, 1936

One keeps hearing in the church that it is all about the tension between God and the devil. But I cannot believe this; it is too convenient a way to deal with one's guilty conscience. The heart does not accuse the devil. In the process of *cor accusator* and *deus defensor* there are only two partners. If one thinks of the cross, there are only two!

—Sunday (Invocavit), March 1, 1936

The morning bathed in brightness, haze, scented air, and the heaviness of summer. I work. Excerpting, sorting, organizing, selecting, one gets quite dizzy from it all. That which deals with the emotion, thought, the religious aspect has been tackled long ago, as a work phase that lies way in the past. What remains is the merciless dilemma of mastering the material and constructing it.

What a word I encountered: "It is not as important to talk with people about God as it is to talk with God about people"! For when talking about God the speaker still retains so much self-elevation. I found this word in a story about the pastor's house; and such words throw the steering wheel around!

The increasing conflict in the church where the declared unity of the nation is falling apart before the eyes of the entire world is kept completely quiet by the press.

—Thursday (Feast of John the Baptist), June 24, 1937

He reveals deep and hidden things.—Daniel 2:22

Two things press on me each day with invariable intensity: the unstoppable progression of time which will transfigure into ultimate fulfillment and the changing face of each day of a new week, despite the most well-structured routine.

No matter what the research will yield in the areas of astronomy, geology, biology, anthropology: Jesus Christ's death and resurrection has to remain the center of time!

—Thursday, July 29, 1937

Peace to this house!—Luke 10:5

The worship service for the 700th anniversary celebration [of Berlin] missed out on the opportunities for a solemn sermon in a metropolitan city: the cloud of witnesses in this godless city Berlin; the [many] hymns that were composed here; the stories in the Bible about big cities. During these times, a good portion of the responsibilities of the office of preaching and the church's tradition seems be falling on the shoulders of poets, and one can only pray for a vast crowd of such messengers of the gospel; for the type of authors that are flocked around the Protestant [magazine] "Eckart" and the Roman Catholic [magazine] "Hochland" will not do, either in terms of quantity or quality. —Sunday, August 15, 1937

The new book [on Martin Luther and Katharina von Bora] is consuming me again, is draining me more than all the dealings with the state ministries; the book, of which Hanni says: "This topic should have stood at the end of your life because no other one could ever be your theme." In the history of the home [lies] the history of the development of the German Bible: the Bible as the ultimate possession—and this at a time when the Bible is so heavily debated and homes are being built as never before.

As difficult as this book will be, as many demands as it will make, as much suffering as it will bring, along with putting at risk my entire existence, being so difficult again for its unpredictability, about the choice of this theme there can be no doubt.

All writing is response to God's most pressing direct speech. The Bible and the home in light of the [political] threats reminiscent of the end times: that was the theme of the past years, and still is? —Monday, August 16, 1937

I see repeatedly that, despite my artistic autonomy, I cannot start anything properly unless it comes from the church's proclamation. What are all words unless they are grounded in the Word, as the Gospel of John calls it? What are all books unless they unmistakably derive their authority, blessing, and validity from the one book which alone is what makes the office of writing so great? . . .

There is Luther, whose experiences I, too, have had from boyhood on with the painful "*volo, sed non possum,*" which I have seen unfold in and dominate my life (to deny that would be ingratitude); [and] the stages of faith—the beginning one, the progressing one, and the perfected one. The first [stage] derives from miracles and signs or some great acts of God; the second believes the mere word without signs and acts; one can gain such a faith only by living it in the bitterness of experience; the third, the perfected faith, presents itself without signs and words; it does not have anything specific it believes because it believes more than could be put into words or proposed; it receives all that is and happens as if it originated with God and it relates it all back to God and to the things that are invisible: "The just shall live by faith."

—Sunday, August 22, 1937

For the first time at a high feast day, I don't feel festive in my heart and home or even at church. This could definitely mean that all inner and outer effort of the will cannot help here. But the spirit of Pentecost has to be victor. God has always made himself known in my home, even during the most difficult times. May he also do it this time, even if everything passes by me as behind thick veils!

The "Midday Song" I finished rhyming only today and gave to Bore [Hanni] for Pentecost. After [writing] new hymns, there comes a peace that always fills the heart, also the senses and the nerves.   —Pentecost Sunday, June 5, 1938

From the Protestant hymnal, Evangelisches Gesangbuch, *a hymn Klepper wrote in 1938, which is included under the category "Fear and Trust":*

Yes, I want to bear you
up until old age,
and you shall give witness
to my gracious ways.

Do not age too early,
give to me your pain;
trust like child would parent,
though your hair be gray.

If I make a promise
I'll make good on it,
bearing you with caring:
You may calmly rest.

Always will I bear you
as a savior would.
Who has seen me failing
where the faithful stood?

Think of former ages
when with steadfastness
I did lead the nations
wanting but their best.

Think of former moments
of the miraculous,
ways and means drew near you
leveling your path.

Lay aside your doubting,
help will always come.
Yes, I want to bear you
as I've always done.

During Sunday worship at St. Nikolassee Church, the con-
gregation sang a hymn by Johann Walter (1496-1570), music
director in Torgau and Dresden and a consultant of Martin
Luther's on matters of liturgy and the revised mass. The hymn,
whose sixth stanza Klepper quotes, is titled "Wake up, Wake
up, you German Lands" and was written in 1561.

> God seeks to warn us evermore;
> the signs tell of this fact,
> for punishment lies at the door;
> so, Germany, react:
> Turn soft and do repent;
> God still intends to give you grace
> and offer you his hand.

For the first time since 1933 I hear a sermon about Christianity, Judaism, and being German; from the old Pastor Kannenberg, who is filling in for Pastor Kurzreiter on his last Sunday of vacation. It spoke to me very much, especially since it was only this week that Hanni decided to be baptized. The sermon said that conversions for the sake of assimilation are no longer happening because what matters now is only race and not Christian membership. But if one or the other Jew was choosing to be baptized right now, this was the only visible sign currently that God had not yet forsaken the people of his old covenant even in Germany and was still drawing individuals to him. —Sunday, August 21, 1938

"A patient person is better than a strong one."
Increasing restrictions for Jews even in hotels. To travel is nearly impossible, other than to go from one private home to another. Since January 1, all Jews, whether baptized or not, have to have as their second given name the name "Israel," all

Jewesses as their second given name "Sara." The list of given names that is prescribed for newborn Jewish children is to eighty percent a sadistic mockery.

The biblical, well-known names are not allowed to Jews. Naturally we took it all in without complaining. The German nation is not behind it. And the Jews—and Hanni, who is remarkably composed and strong—are fearing much worse: deportation without any of their possessions. With each worried thought about the future, Hanni and I are taking a grateful look at God's guidance in the past. And since Hanni wants to become a Christian I am much calmer. God had spoken so clearly.

Since the conference at Evian has made it clear that other countries are not willing to help German Jews, everything has become even more tragic.

"Powerlessness" and "overcoming" in the sense of Romans 8:37-39, these have been the poles of my thought during these last months.   —Tuesday, August 23, 1938

In a letter to Professor Rudolf Hermann

Thank you for [sending] the Luther lectures held at Wittenberg, which fit so well into my work, so that I am again your pupil. Beyond that I am gratified by such needful sentences as: "Too much ado about eschatology during these times of great change!" and "Is it not true that such contemporary interpretations of the end times tend to come and go?" Once again I would ask that you would let me know if anything should change in your assessment of the CC [Confessing Church]. I no longer grasp that situation and don't want to be unfair toward those of the CC who continue to woo me so intently. I cannot yet overcome my resistance toward it, since I see in the CC a man-made and largely political undertaking and an effort to divide that lacks a commission and its necessity. I was taken aback by the fact that they wanted from me "battle hymns" and that they should consider as so important the membership of an author like me. All that seems to me a "delegating" of the use of gifts that is manufactured by humans and stands in contrast to 1 Corinthians 12 [on the use of spiritual gifts] and Ephesians 4 [on the offices in the church]. . . .

The book project of "The Eternal Home," of which I am fonder than that of "The Father," is a great burden especially during these times. Yet, as paradoxical as this may sound, I believe that one is ultimately carried by the very thing one regards as one's greatest burden. Because when it comes to the burden, God most certainly will not abandon us there. Only a hundred pages have been written of the new book. I am quite weary of a separate introduction to Luther, though it is not possible to write about him solely through the mirror of Katharina von Bora's life, even if one describes her relationship with him, her home, and her estate.

You wrote, most reverend Professor, of the growing experience with all that seems to hinder one's work. This is true. The words [of Luther], "If they take body, home, honor, child, and spouse" and the circumstances that prompted their writing, I am able to grasp only now. What great danger there is, especially for our Renate, who is still living with us.

—Berlin-Nikolassee, January 23, 1940

Renerle [Renate]. In her new school she is already everyone's darling. All prayers end in what concerns her future.

Again and again, Hanni and I were compelled to look at the incredibly beautiful sun down above the yard. Even where everything appears like a departure, a loss, uncertainty, God still gives and gives.

Our small piano has been tuned for Christmas; I will take advantage of it for the Advent hymns.

The wood of our own trees, felled with the [house] construction, is all split and piled up; for this winter of the war, Bore has made preparations with such faithfulness and cleverness and diligence. There is so much heaviness in the heart—but much more trust and gratitude. Now it's time to prepare the Bora material that is being worked on currently so it can be returned [to the library]. . . .

There is no "Stop!" from God that is not also a call to repentance—proclaiming that the heavenly kingdom wants to draw near! —Wednesday, November 27, 1940

I will sing to the Lord, because he has dealt bountifully with me.—Psalm 13:6

It is so strange and earth-shattering: the great, heavy question after one's own new beginning is irrevocably tied to the question of the future of the church at the end of the war. It has become the essential question of life for us. And it has become the question about Germany. Things look bleak for the church: the domes at Braunschweig and Naumburg have been annexed [by the state] for secular celebrations, are no longer available for worship.

The young theologians, male and female, who as of yet lack a regular place of employment and who like the many vicars of the Confessing Church cannot find one, are being retrained for "service for the common good."

The Nazi commissioner of the Warthe region declares with pride that there is no church left there.
　　　　　　　　　　　　　—Thursday, November 28, 1940

The fact that Jewish women in mixed marriages [married to an Aryan] are spared the wearing of a yellow star makes one quietly receive such "an act of equality."

I found tickets for a Brahms concert at the Philharmonic.

Most certainly, there continues, apart from what is happening, also a true cultural life during the war. If only it were not paralleled by nameless, mute tragedy and disaster.

Yes, I have seen the doom of the nations and stand quite close to the mystical tragedy of the people whom God once chose as his. Does this people have to do penance all alone? Will God save this people by making it like Christ by its "innocent and vicarious suffering"? Is God carrying out his plan among the Jews by means of the Jewish Christians, whose outward fate is no different from that of the other Jews? Though one hears of difficulties they have with the others.

—Sunday, October 12, 1941

We know what suicide would mean in our case: three-fold murder, disobedience to God, losing one's patience, flight from the providence of God, triumph of the negative forces innate to humans, discarding trust [in God].

But it is not the unforgivable sin against the Holy Spirit; it is no more than the sin that the Christian drags along as the *fortiter pecca* until the end. How our life is a bad witness for God all the way to the end! I know no Christian who is truly "sanctified." . . .

In all this there is no breaking with God, despite the willingness to commit terrible sin. The sin to come in our life is certainly no less.

Perhaps I am also burdened by having to continue to work; but it's not the worry, which would certainly be justified, that the kind of books I write are no longer permitted to be published. This is true for all other Christian authors.

The radical solution of the Jewish question, the confiscation of monasteries, the dissolving of Christian schools, the possibility of killing "unworthy" life—all this is happening now—as the army is in the field. Afterwards, the officers can wash their hands of any guilt. Even this bridge has been diabolically built. . . .

The child [Renate] is accepting of whatever comes and still hopes that things will pass. Hanni is so busy, so diligent, so grateful that she no longer has to worry about me. But it is a big disappointment for both of us that to Renerle the thought of suicide is not drawing closer but moving farther away. It is Renerle—her courage to live, which produces faith—who is preventing our suicide. —Monday, October 20, 1941

One of Klepper's hymns in the Protestant hymnal, Evangelisches Gesangbuch, *is included under the rubric "Dying and Eternal Life"; the hymn was written in 1941.*

> The heart releases what it held:
> its gladness, goods, and land;
> Come, Holy Spirit, Comforter,
> grant solace from God's hand.
>
> The heart makes peace with all
> the heaviness endured;
> come, Savior, do connect with us,
> our wounds help bear and cure.
>
> The heart soars toward you,
> is borne by you and raised.
> Come, Father, stay with us, for then
> lament turns into praise!

At nine in the morning it was still dark and veiled as we prepared the gift-giving for Hanni; the birthday setting is especially beautiful this year, this so serious year: the small, fine Empire mirror for the hallway, in front of it the early and plain Baroque chair with its faded pink velvet, the luscious, fine Renaissance wall light fixtures from a church, the plethora of cyclamen, asters, the half-round of the candles amidst the tender green vines. . . . Lit candles on the breakfast table with its primulas, old porcelain—but soon the mild sunlight entered the rooms facing the garden, covered the birthday table. . . . Bore's birthday and Reformation Day coincide this year, which meant that the worship service for Hanni's birthday had all the great hymns and the great liturgy.

—Hanni's Birthday, Sunday, November 2, 1941

Through Prince Georg [a Jesuit] I hear about events that place my dismissal [from the army] into a new light. Concurrently with us men in mixed marriages and the sons of mixed marriages have been also dismissed the Jesuits, who only recently had been drafted, and twenty-one princes of the houses Hohenzollern, Wettin, Wittelsbach, and Habsburg, before they could have been promoted! . . . Prince Georg looks a lot more discouraged than before. The royal lineage in this priest is unmistakable. Catholicism is steadily growing in intensity. At least in the most prominent officers of the new army, the famous captains Mölders and Galland, Catholicism has found two courageous defenders. If only there were more: they would be a force.

Things have developed in such a way that one utters a loud sigh—unawares.

Prelate [Bernhard] Lichtenberg, who prayed in St. Hedwig's Church for the Catholic Jews, has been arrested.

—Tuesday, November 4, 1941

The news, as of yet unconfirmed, reached us that the actor Joachim Gottschalk has committed suicide with his Jewish wife after he had first put to death his children. He had been barred from the film industry and his stage-acting was thought to be next.

I feel as though I am working only because it gives Hanni such great comfort, since all she wants is that I write, even if it is no longer meant for this time.

And there are no more hymn texts coming to me!

—Monday, November 10, 1941

In the evening, the child sits often by me, something she rarely did before; but she is always very tired.

Even Hanni has reached the point where she cries—she who never cried, not even at my departure, nor at Brigitte's departure—at the sight of Jewish children, of young or old Jews as they are heading out so visibly scared in their helpless doings. In [the Nazi paper] *Reich* is a horrible article, titled "It's the Jews' Fault," and its occasion is obvious: the population's sympathy in light of the yellow star and the deportations.

—Friday, November 14, 1941

I was able to spend a good amount of time alone with Hilde and go over the last will with her, the instructions that one half of our estate was to go to Brigitte and the other half to Hilde herself. Hilde did come through.

—Friday, December 5, 1941

God is no longer asking about the "Eternal Home"; I have been released of it all in an ominous way; I am simply no longer able to work. . . .

The child, the child! What is everything else by comparison!

There is one Bible passage after another that one is no longer able to say, such as: "I will not die but live and proclaim the works of the Lord."

But we are being led ever more deeply into the prayer of the Our Father: "And lead us not into temptation."

Mysterious is that one is able to be glad of everything beautiful and good one still encounters.

Three of Renerle's colleagues have been ordered for the next deportation on January 6. What a Christmas for these baptized Jews, now that they have been notified of this date!

—Wednesday, December 17, 1941

In mid-October 1942, the couple went on a week-long trip to Johanna's hometown, Nuremberg, also visiting Würzburg, and Augsburg. Nineteen-year-old Renate stayed at home. In early December, Katharina was born to daughter Brigitte in England.

Daily, hourly the burden pressing down upon the nations and the Jews becomes so oppressive and threatening that I am almost relieved that the dissonance created by the trip has ended. But Hanni is so grateful for the little that had been offered her by the trip.

It is no longer a time one could meet with action; it is a time of sighing and bearing things, and the gaze up to God becomes increasingly shy.

Today arrived from Augsburg the Christ extending a blessing which is my Christmas gift for Hanni. To see this statue again while unwrapping it in the basement was moving.

One is surrounded by such peace, such beauty; has made such a luxurious trip: how can one—must one—be so dizzy, so numb, so tired and confused and downcast.

—Thursday, November 5, 1942

In reference to a line from Martin Luther's hymn "A Mighty Fortress," translated into English as "Let goods and kindred go, this mortal life also":

God knows that I am not able to allow Hanni and the child to go into this most brutal and most horrid of deportations. He knows that I am unable to give him this promise the way Luther did: "If they take the body, goods, honor, child, and wife, let them all go." Body, goods, honor—yes! God also knows that I would accept every test and every sentence, as long as I know that Hanni and the child are more or less safe. . . .

I am still writing this in hopes that I might read it again and look back on the path of my life, God's path with me.

But what has begun is no longer unfathomable. In a terrible way it has entered our consciousness.

A dark, stormy, mild, overcast day—like fading and dissipating fate.

God is bigger than our heart.—The Word will be accompanying us into death.   —Tuesday, December 8, 1942

Tomorrow at three I have been asked to meet again with the ministry for the interior. Since on the phone I can only say very little, Hilde came over after work. Now everything that we had to burden her with during last year's Advent has drawn so close.

These still, still, dark, overcast days. So mild, so full of heaven's sorrow.

"When the Lord restored the fortunes of Zion, we were like those who dream" [Psalm 126:1].

Yet one more day of agonizing wait. And yet, everything moves so quickly. In the evening, poor Hilde at our place to go over our last will.

Hanni's poor heart grieves about "The Eternal Home." Brigitte—Katharina.   —Wednesday, December 9, 1942

In the afternoon the meeting at the ministry for the interior. We are dying now—alas, this too is valid before God—

This evening we are walking into death together.

Over us stands during the last hours the image of Christ extending his blessing, wrestling for us.

Under his gaze our life ends.

—Thursday, December 10, 1942

SOURCES

Klepper, Jochen. 1957. *Unter dem Schatten deiner Flügel: Aus den Tagebüchern der Jahre 1932-1942.* Foreword by Reinhold Schneider. Ed. Hildegard Klepper. Stuttgart: Deutsche Verlags-Anstalt.

———. 1973. *Briefwechsel 1925-1942.* Ed. Ernst G. Riemschneider. Stuttgart: Deutsche Verlags-Anstalt.

Evangelisches Gesangbuch. 1996. Gütersloh: Gütersloher Verlagshaus.

Bernhard Lichtenberg
(1875-1943)

Cathedral Provost in Berlin

During the "Reichskristallnacht" on the eve of November 9, 1938, the Nazi regime launched a systematic raid on Jewish businesses, homes, and synagogues. Throughout Germany, nearly two hundred synagogues went up in flames, and more than 7,000 Jewish stores were ransacked and demolished in the attack. Only a thousand meters away from the Nazi headquarters in Berlin, the pastor of Berlin's St. Hedwig Cathedral discovered in the early morning the vandalism and the smashed storefront windows. "What happened yesterday we know. What will happen tomorrow we don't know. But what has happened today we have experienced ourselves," he said during evening prayer in the cathedral. "The temple outside is in flames. And it, too, is a house of God." From that day on, daily for three years, he would risk being arrested for inviting the faithful to join him in prayer: "Let us pray for the persecuted non-Aryan Christians and the Jews." Denounced by two visiting students in August of 1941, the priest was arrested a month later, put on trial, and incarcerated at Tegel prison for two years, then deported to a concentration camp. Seriously ill and weakened by starvation, he died during transport. In

1996, *John Paul II canonized him, and in 2004 the Holocaust Memorial Society Yad Vashem declared him a "righteous among the nations."*

Blessed Bernhard Lichtenberg was born on December 3, 1875, in Ohlau, near Breslau. He grew up the eldest of four boys. The family belonged to the Catholic minority in the city and owned a fine foods store, connected with a wine tavern whose corner table was designated for political discussions among Roman Catholics. Early on, the boy showed interest in religious matters and practiced a dedicated piety. Each day the mother took him with her to church. His love for music and singing, horse-back riding, and gymnastics was coupled with oratorical skills and an inviolate character, albeit a tendency to rashness. After graduating from the gymnasium, Lichtenberg began his theological studies at the University of Innsbruck. The separation from the mother was hard for him, leading to daily correspondence by letter where the son gave glimpses into his long hours of study and austere lifestyle, and the mother urged moderation and leniency. After one semester, Lichtenberg returned to Silesia to complete his studies for the priesthood at the University of Breslau. He was ordained a priest in 1899. For three years, he served smaller parishes, first in Neisse, also called the "Silesian Rome," then in the working-class parish of Friedrichsberg-Lichtenberg, near Berlin and later part of the city. By then, Berlin had grown from half a million residents sixty years earlier to over two million, of whom only 10 percent were Catholics. Shortage of employment forced factory workers and day laborers into moldy tenements and squalid barracks, contrasting sharply with the city's expansive boulevards and promenades, grandiose theaters and opera houses, and luxurious patrician villas.

During the two years in Friedrichsberg-Lichtenberg, the newly ordained priest became acquainted with ministry in the rather secular, anti-Catholic climate of a bustling metropolis. His mentor and pastor there was Nikolaus Kuborn, who had planted and built the "diaspora" church St. Mauritius. After Lichtenberg was transferred to Berlin-Charlottenburg, he returned for the next twenty years to make weekly confession and share meals with his former pastor. Work had been hard in the small, fledgling parish that Pastor Kuborn had built. No more than fifty people attended mass in the half-finished church building of St. Mauritius, mostly elderly, hard of hearing women. Undeterred by cynical and skeptical comments, Lichtenberg reached out through pastoral visits dressed in his floor-length cassock and equipped with a small silver bell in one hand and a red lit lamp of the Eucharistic presence in the other. When riding on the newly opened subway, he would make the sign of the cross before reading his breviary. And before descending the train, he would wish his seat neighbor farewell with a hearty "Praised be Jesus Christ!" The requisite "Heil Hitler," standard greeting during the Nazi era, never came from his lips.

Lichtenberg's ministry was marked by self-denying discipline, charitable giving, and a passion for helping souls. An incisive, quick-witted public speaker and energetic preacher, he would draw large crowds with his sermons, even if metaphors and story lines were predictable and delivery akin to the modulated voice of a Shakespearean actor. Smaller prayer gatherings would have him switch from chancel to organ bench, from where he played a hymn and led the congregation in song. His flock sensed that beneath the thundering preaching and singing voice beat the heart of a man steeped in prayer, who believed every word he said and walked his talk. Children in the poor workers' quarters flocked to this old-fashioned catechesis teacher calling him lovingly behind his back "the pope," while the grief-stricken, sick, and troubled received comfort and spiritual guidance by his unwavering attentiveness. "I was far away from God," an elderly woman recalled. "He converted me. He was always good to me like a father, was completely with God." Many of his meditations and gatherings for prayer closed with the words "May there ever come to pass, be praised, and eternally honored the most sweet, holy, and righteous will of God, unfathomable in its heights and depths, now and forevermore. Amen."

As chaplain and missioner in Berlin, Lichtenberg served several parishes. He also founded a number of new ones by making new converts, planting the seed of the gospel through preaching, catechesis, and administering the sacraments, and by raising funds for the building of churches. Lichtenberg sent off hundreds of soliciting letters to addresses throughout Germany and Switzerland, raised money as a substitute preacher in neighboring parishes, and turned his annual vacations into begging trips. By hiking through Silesia and Westphalia, traveling to Baden and Wuerttemberg, and crisscrossing the Rhineland and Switzerland, he brought in additional funds and helped recruit personnel in support of the next building project or mission. Why look to Africa and Asia when "Berlin is worth a few missionaries?" he asked men and women religious in his audience, including those gathered at the 1926 Eucharistic World Conference in Chicago. Lichtenberg helped found five new parishes in Berlin-Charlottenburg, allowing him in time to move worship services into a church from spaces previously leased at a school, office building, or racetrack.

In addition to his pastoral duties, Lichtenberg carried out several auxiliary functions. For four years during World War I he served as chaplain to soldiers and prisoners of war in the city, then became involved in Berlin's political arena. Between 1919 and 1931, he was an elected district official and member of the labor-friendly, later Centrist party. Unlike today,

Catholic clergy were not prohibited from holding political office; rather, they were encouraged to act, after Bismarck's "culture war," as a force in the recovery of Christian values in Germany's social and economic life. Lichtenberg fought for the rights of the Catholic minority: He lobbied for adding religious instruction for Catholic children to the public school curriculum (since Protestant instruction was already available) and the rezoning of church property so homes could be built on it for large Catholic families. Having studied Hitler's book Mein Kampf and annotated it with critical, biting margin notations, Lichtenberg felt compelled to denounce, during political gatherings, the Nazi hate propaganda against Jews and the Jesuit order. When, during public debates, Catholics were portrayed as mindless vassals of Rome and sympathizers of violence, or when freethinkers lobbied for the removal of antiabortion laws, Lichtenberg spoke up, either alone or in concert with men he had brought along from his parish. On one occasion, his stalwart opposition earned him death treats from the enraged crowd.

When the Pacifist League of German Catholics ("Friedens-bund deutscher Katholiken") protested against a nationalist militarism and the glorification of war, Lichtenberg was an active member. And when in 1929 the league joined forces with Protestant and other religious organizations in forming the League of Denominations for Peace ("Vereinigung der Konfessionen für den Frieden"), Lichtenberg was an elected member of the board. It was this same Pacifist League that in 1931 sponsored the public viewing of the American antiwar, antimilitaristic film All Quiet on the Western Front, based on a novel by Erich Maria Remarque. The showing was danger-ous, given that the secret police had prohibited its screening in movie theaters. The movie dramatically portrayed, from the perspective of the common soldier, the butcher-like atmosphere *of war and the deathly fallacies of militaristic ideals. With Lichtenberg's signature on the invitation, he received heaps of anonymous hate mail calling him "You pig, bastard of a priest, Jew lover, traitor, low life!" And the* Angriff, *a paper published by Hitler's propaganda minister Paul Joseph Goebbels, called Lichtenberg's support of the movie "a mocking of the war's dead soldiers" and demanded: "Out, throw him out, this Monsignor Lichtenberg!"*

In 1913, Lichtenberg began serving as pastor of the Herz-Jesu Parish in Charlottenburg, where his pastoral ministry went hand in hand with his social engagement on behalf of the city's Catholic minority. When appointed canon at the newly founded cathedral chapter of St. Hedwig's in 1931, he resigned from political office. The following year, he became cathedral dean and in 1937 cathedral provost, a position that involved overseeing the direction of the chapter, serving as its official spokesperson, and being in charge of liturgical ceremonies in the absence of the bishop. Lichtenberg was responsible for the affairs of men and women religious in the diocese. He served as chaplain to various diocesan organizations. And he helped oversee the work of various charitable organizations, such as the League of the Cross, which cared for alcoholics and their families, and the Catholic Charitable League for Women, Girls, and Children. In 1938, his bishop put Lichtenberg in charge of the newly founded diocesan Relief Office of Berlin, whose task it was to assist Catholics of Jewish descent in emigrating from the Third Reich, first openly, then, during the war years, covertly.

Between September 1938 and March 1939, more than 3,500 visitors seeking help came to the diocesan Relief Office for baptized Jews, housed on the property of Lichtenberg's former parish, the Herz-Jesu Church. Another 2,000 letters arrived in the mail during that time, as did between fifty and seventy phone calls a day. The Relief Office provided legal counsel, money and food stamps, placement into war-related jobs so deportation was deemed "unpractical," assistance with emigration and support of the deported with packages and money, along with running a school for Protestant and Catholic children of Jewish descent who had been banned from public schools. But Lichtenberg was not satisfied with helping only Jews that had been baptized; he also wanted to help Jews who were not. In that he enlisted the assistance of numerous confidantes and liaisons, including that of the Vatican: via courier the diocesan Relief Office had informed the pope of the harsh treatment of Jews and their mass deportation from Berlin.

When a leaflet of October 23, 1941, effectively prohibited Jews from emigrating and Germans from extending help or showing any form of kindness to Jews, Lichtenberg prepared an appeal he planned to read from the chancel of St. Hedwig's on the upcoming Sunday: a protest against racial hatred and murder, and an admonition to parishioners to show neighborly love to the suffering and persecuted Jews in the name of Christ. He never was able to do so. Arrested by the secret police on October 25, Lichtenberg was interrogated, put in detention, tried in May 1942, and sentenced to two years in prison. On March 1, 1943, St. Hedwig's Cathedral was destroyed during a bomb attack. When told about it, the prisoner Lichtenberg remarked, "That means little compared to the deportation of 2,000 Jews the night before." Despite his heart troubles since the summer of 1938 and an infected kidney, Lichtenberg remained at Tegel prison between May 1942 and October 1943, lacking proper medical attention. During transport to the Dachau concentration camp, he died at the city hospital of Hof/Saale on November 5. Following a pontifical requiem mass, Lichtenberg's body was buried at St. Hedwig Cemetery. In 1965, his remains were exhumed and transferred to the crypt of the rebuilt St. Hedwig's Cathedral in Berlin. John Paul II stepped in when the Vatican's fact-finding process for canonization, begun in 1967, seemed to linger. In 1994, the pope announced that Lichtenberg's status as a martyr for Christ was undeniable. No one would have been more surprised than Lichtenberg when John Paul II declared him "blessed" on June 23, 1996, during a ceremony at Berlin's Olympic stadium.

* * *

Lichtenberg's papers and most of his diaries, letters, and sermons have been lost. Primary sources survive in the form of an early biography (1946), official Nazi trial documents, eyewitness accounts, and public records and newspaper articles.

During his studies at the Catholic seminary in Breslau, Lichtenberg recorded in his diary what had a lasting impact on his life. While at the Breslau Cathedral, he heard the cantor sing Psalm 62, which he would later regard as this "endless confession valid for all times and peoples." Looking back on the experience forty years later, he writes in 1941: "I would like to write a book, only one and it should be called: Deus, Deus meus, ad te de luce vigilo, and whoever reads it should always find joy in the fact that he or she is allowed daily to wake up to our dear Lord."

[I went] as a young student to the dome at Breslau during matins and lauds. And a dome vicar began to sing Psalm 62: Deus, Deus meus, ad Te de luce vigilo. To you, my God, I wake up in the morning. At the time I knew little about the translation and interpretation of Psalms, just as I don't know much about it now; but I could hear the joy resulting from the fact that a human soul was waking up in the morning to God and that this God is my God—and very often after that I could suddenly hear this "Deus, Deus meus" in the dark dome and could see the bright, solemn notes rising up to the apse and could feel them." —*Er widerstand*, p. 47.

His impressions from his time at the seminary

When the group of ninety [seminarians] gathered for the first time in their robes, each one experienced the sacred clothing as a symbol of obligation. It was a completely new awakening to God when Father Rector solemnly gave the seminarians the ten-day exercises, concluding with a general confession of one's entire life. Such a general confession has to be a true ending after which comes the new construction. If this last year of seminary is to be a lasting, comforting memory into old age, the soul has to be calm; then the exercise of jointly praying the breviary becomes a blessed revelation . . . the muted sound the bishop's crosier calls forth from knocking at the old tombs, the jubilant Salve Regina carried high by the angelic-sounding voice of the boys choir, truth, piety, and beauty allowed the soul to resound and subside like in a three-voice harmony when afterwards the experiences in the dome came alive again in the solitary room of the seminarian. "I am never less alone than when I am alone, because when I am not by myself I am with people, and when I am by myself I am with God."

During his "involuntary two-year penance" in prison, Lichtenberg sees himself as a contemplative Carthusian monk in his cell, reminiscent of his small room at the seminary.

One would wish a single room for every seminarian and every woman religious. During the time of preparation for the priestly office at least, each seminarian should become a Carthusian monk. Such a quiet, small, high-ceilinged room that one can traverse with a few long strides, barefoot, the way Dr. Kneipp would recommend, while respectful of the person living one floor below, is ideal for meditation; by the window is the high-boy desk, where one receives one's thoughts; the view through the window does not distract because it leads into a court, enclosed on all sides and with a solitary tree; . . . a wardrobe, a table, a bed, a chair, and now this room is my abode where I will experience the preparation for tonsure and lower orders, the minor diaconate and the diaconate and finally ordination to the priesthood. Visitors will not bother me; only Father Prior will check up on the seminarian every so often, and only when the bell tolls will I leave my quiet cell and always return to it with gladness, be it from the garden or the school or the refectory or from a trip to town.

—*Er widerstand*, pp. 48-49.

From his travel diary dated December 17, 1925, while on a tour through southern Germany

For supper a piece of dry bread with bad beer. Afterwards Anton brought over a liverwurst. With kerosene lamp and three matches upstairs, freezing cold, dirty bed covered with big pieces of newspaper, taken off mittens and then stretched out. The hot-water bottle spilled and I lay in water! Out of bed, match doesn't work, another bed next door, dripping wet into it and fallen asleep. The next day getting dressed in the dark, light, to church, sitting down in the pew. Hartmann L. comes to orate mass which I celebrate coram sanctissimo [with the Blessed Sacrament on exposition]. One hour of catechesis, back across the Main, then to Bamberg and to Charlottenburg. There at nine o' clock in the evening. At home. Deo gratias!"

—*Wer glaubt, muss widerstehen*, p. 44.

Decades after his ordination to the priesthood, Lichtenberg recalls:

And tomorrow I will return to my home town, and Father

and Mother—for a long time both have been resting next to each other at the Herz-Jesu Cemetery in the Marchan sand—will embrace the son who is now a priest and he will, dressed in priestly clothes, kneel down before them and ask for their blessing, and then the priest who had prepared him for his first communion will lead him to the altar, and a priest friend of the parents will give the ordination homily in the same chancel where he said during the *Kulturkampf*: "A priest remains a priest, and even if he were in chains and bonds," a word that cost him his freedom and brought him imprisonment and a flight to Rome. And then there will come during the F-Flat Mass of Brosig a very quiet moment where for the first time will take place by God's might in [my] Fridolin's hands the miracle that once occurred in the womb of the Virigin; and then the gilded paten in his left hand will tremble when with his right he beats his guilt-ridden breast and says in a shaky voice: Domine, non sum dignus. And the following Saturday a farm wagon will stop at the door of the parents' home and take him to the Thomas Church; there he will for the first time absolve the first penitent at the confessional grate and proclaim to the villagers the Word of God and chant the High Office, and another week later he will be the substitute officiant at a baptism: Deus, Deus meus, ad Te de luce vigilo."

—*Er widerstand*, p. 50.

About his year at the parish in Neisse

A happy awakening took place in the parish when the 46th General Conference of German Catholics convened in Neisse. The speeches have gone silent, the decorations are dried up—but the soul wakes up again and again to God when recalling the greeting to the assembly of the president, Justice Minister Dr. Spahn: "Praised be Jesus Christ" and the thousands respectfully standing there respond by professing with one voice: "Forever and ever. Amen."   —*Er widerstand*, p. 53.

On March 1, 1935, a former theology student entered St. Hedwig's Cathedral and scattered the sacred host that was being kept in the tabernacle. Having read anti-Catholic literature, the student declared that the Catholic rites were nothing but idol worship. The bishop called for penitential services to rein in the "godless and anti-Christian literature." On March 28, Lichtenberg orders that all clergy in the diocese of Berlin offer up for the following two weeks "prayer against the forces of darkness."

Lord and Savior Jesus Christ! See, the forces of darkness are fighting against the children of light. False prophets and antichrists have risen up who are removing from the people the sacred teaching and are numbing them with fables, myths, and enchanting words. In the midst of this dangerous confusion of minds, we need, O Lord, the light of your truth and the power of your mercy. We beg you, fill the preachers during passion week with the spirit of your great apostle, so that with apostolic insight and in apostolic freedom they may find the right words to say in order to bring their listeners to the realization that you, O Lord, are the truth and the life and that the church is the Führerin [leader] ordained by you for our eternal paths."
—*Er widerstand*, p. 93.

On May 18, 1935, at St. Hedwig's, Lichtenberg officiated at a requiem mass for the Polish army marshal and dictator Jozef Pilsudski. Hitler, who had revered the dictator, was present. Exactly two months later, Lichtenberg filed a complaint with the Prussian Ministry protesting the human rights abuses at the concentration camp Esterwegen. Informed of these abuses by a written report and unable to reach the Prussian president of ministry by phone, Lichtenberg signed the report himself with the request for an "examination and remedy" of the matter.

On April 13, 1935, the leader of the German Miners Union and formerly a member of parliament of the Social Democratic Party Fritz Husemann was shot to death at Camp Esterwegen. Fourteen days later the communist Röhrs (Rövers?) of Bremen was shot (two shots into the neck) while working outside. The day after, the body was laid out in the storage alley in a wooden box in dirty, unwashed, blood-smeared condition dressed in the worker's uniform. The inmates had to line up and march in file past the body of the shot comrade. The first in line expressed their respects by taking off their hats. That was stopped with the cries: "The expressions of respect have to stop, of all things to greet a swine like that." Because of these happenings, the Jewish painter Loewy lost his head. The next day while working outside he simply walked off. He was shot. A little after that the communist Ohl of Frankfurt am Main tried to hang himself. He was caught in the act and cut loose in time. As punishment he received twenty-five beatings with a cane. The following day while going outside to work, Ohl was gunned down. The Jews especially are made to suffer. Mostly they have to haul sewage and clean the toilet pits, sometimes with their bare hands. When commanded to roll over, they have to roll in the manure.   —*Er widerstand*, p. 100.

In a letter to Adolf Hitler of December 10, 1935, Lichtenberg protests the Nazi Party's allowing smear campaigns against the church.

May I be permitted to most respectfully inform the Führer and Chancellor Adolf Hitler that the newsstands are selling the "Pfaffenspiegel," distributed at a circulation of 1.25 million copies, largely on account of Social Democrat [efforts], which has destroyed many people's respect for the priesthood and the church. . . . As cathedral provost of St. Hedwig's parish, which also includes the chancellor's offices, I feel entitled to submit the direct request to the Führer and Chancellor to stop the work of these journalistic gravediggers of our German homeland.

—*Er widerstand*, pp. 95-96.

At a speech in Aachen on December 10, 1939, the theologian Karl Adam postulated a uniquely "German ethos," based on "the demands of the German blood, the German history," and he called for "military service of Catholic theologians," a German-language liturgy, and the distinct veneration of German saints. Lichtenberg challenges Adam's position.

Why speak of a distinctly German morality? Is it because the German has received on account of "his soil, his climate, his history, his fate, etc. etc." other responsibilities than the resident of a South Sea island? Is morality relative, is there one for the German, another for the resident of the South Sea island? The fact that we have tasks to fulfill that differ from those living on a South Sea island does not change the moral disposition toward these tasks. The false premise of a German world view results in the false view of a German ethos. The entire discourse about a German world view and a German ethos is moving dangerously close to relativism.

—*Er widerstand*, p. 126.

In a letter of August 20, 1941, to the church minister of the Reich, Hanns Kerrl, Lichtenberg sharply criticizes the church politics of the Nazi regime.

But you, Mister Minister of the Reich, are asking as the representative of the state that Catholic bishops fight against the enemy of Christianity and of religion in general when in reality this very state is the fanatical and brutal enemy of Christianity, especially of the Catholic Church and with that of religion in general. Only, it conceals its enmity against Christianity beneath the hypocritical mask of a "positivist Christianity," which is in reality the positive idolizing of the state and differs from Bolshevism only by its cowardly camouflage. For such a diabolical deception, the Führer and the ministers of a Third Reich that has been in existence for less than a decade will be unable to win the bishops of a church that has existed for almost two thousand years. One by one they would rather climb up the [executioner's] scaffold than to dirty their priestly garments with a deceitful patriotism, leading to the downfall of the German people and country.

A week later, on August 28, 1941, Lichtenberg writes a letter to the Reich's medical director, Dr. Conti, protesting the systematic killing of the mentally ill in Germany, as reported by the Bishop of Münster, Clemens August von Galen.

The Bishop of Münster gave a sermon on August 3, 1941, in the St. Lamberti-Church in Münster in which he claimed he had been assured that the ministry of the interior and the offices of the medical director of the Reich, Dr. Conti, are well aware that a large number of the mentally ill in Germany have been intentionally put to death and will continue to be killed in the future. Had this report been false, you, Mister Medical Director of the Reich, would have long ago publicly denounced this preaching bishop and would have sued him, or the secret police would have taken care of him. That has not happened. Thereby you admit that it is true. . . . If the state, charged with prosecuting crime and enforcing punishment of such crime, does not see an occasion to intervene here, then every German citizen, spurred on by his or her conscience and status, is obligated to do so. That is what I am doing right now. [A personal report follows of a woman whose mentally handicapped son had been euthanized by the Nazis.] God only knows how many thousand or ten thousand cases like that have occurred. The public is not allowed to know and, as in this case, the relatives would have to fear for their freedom and lives were they to publicly protest.

My conscience as a priest is held captive by the knowledge of such crimes against moral law and federal law. Even though I am only one person, I demand of you, Mister Medical Director, as a human being, a Christian, a priest, and a German to render an account of these crimes, which have been ordered by you or been committed with your consent, and which are provoking the wrath to come over the German people of the one who alone is Lord of life and death.

I am also copying this letter to the offices of the Reich's chancellor, the ministries, and the secret police.

—*Bernhard Lichtenberg*, p. 46.

The next day, Lichtenberg was again praying during Vespers, saying, "Let us pray for the Jews and for the poor inmates at concentration camps, and most especially for my priestly brothers." Two visiting female students, appalled by the prayer, filed an official complaint. Lichtenberg was arrested on October 25, 1941, and interrogated. During his three-hour trial on May 22, 1942, he was charged with "chancel abuse" and violating the "defamation law" (Heimtückegesetz), which made it a felony to publicly criticize and oppose the Nazi regime. When asked at the trial what had prompted his habit of public intercessory prayer and the particular prayer at St. Hedwig's, he answered:

For the past thirty-six years it has been my habit to hold daily evening prayer at the parish I serve. During such an evening prayer I have always recalled those in particular distress and the needy. For example, when persecution broke out in Mexico, I prayed for the persecuted in Mexico; during the persecution in Russia for the Russian peoples; during the persecution in Spain for the persecuted Christians in Spain. . . . [Similarly I prayed for] the millions of refugees, not knowing their name or citizenship, for the soldiers who were fighting, wounded, and dying here and on the other side, for the bombed cities in allied and enemy territory [and for my own country and the leaders of the German people].

I can tell you exactly [how the evening prayer at St. Hedwig's came about]. It was in November 1938, when the storefront windows were being destroyed and the synagogues burning; there I went through the streets of my parish early in the morning, let's say between 5 and 6 o' clock, prior to saying mass. When I saw the devastation, which the police were watching passively, I was outraged by the vandalism, and I wondered: What can be done here when something like this can happen in an orderly country? And I said to myself: Only one thing can help, prayer. And that evening I prayed for the first time: "Let us pray for the persecuted non-Aryan Christians and for the Jews."   —*Er widerstand*, p. 136.

During his interrogation and while serving his sentence in prison, Lichtenberg repeatedly requested to be sent to the Polish concentration camp in Litzmannstadt (Lodz) as a chaplain to Jews and Jewish Christians. Initially, the secret police agreed to the request knowing full well, as did he, that it would mean the priest's certain death.

[I am opposed to the deportation of the Jews and all it entails] because it goes against the main commandment of Christianity, "You ought to love your neighbor as yourself," and I recognize my neighbor also in the Jew, who has an eternal soul fashioned in the image and likeness of God. Since I could not stop this decree from being carried out, I was determined to accompany deported Jews and Christian Jews into their banishment in order to provide them with pastoral care there. I am using this occasion to ask the secret police to grant this my request.   —*Wer glaubt, muss widerstehen*, p. 117.

While in detention at Moabit and serving his sentence at Tegel prison for abuse of the chancel privilege and violation of the Heimtücke law, Lichtenberg translated and set to meter 147 hymns, drafted 153 sermons, wrote several biographical sketches of the saints, and immersed himself in the study of church history and the Italian language. He also made the spiritual exercises and wrote letters, signing them as "Cathedral Provost B.L., Carthusian Monk." To his bishop, Konrad Cardinal Count von Preysing (bishop of Berlin between 1935 and 1950), Lichtenberg writes on July 5, 1942, from Tegel:

Meanwhile I have become a Carthusian monk who has yet to finish his second year of the novitiate [prison]. In the early morning I am helping our Dear Lady with cleaning up, then off to St. Joseph in the carpenter shop. To my left sits the jar of glue, to my right 1,150 well stacked and glued envelopes. Tomorrow is Holy Mass and Holy Communion. Our cathedral provost would say: "And so on and so forth." Once again I thank you much for the letter of June 22 which I could read only with tears of joy and would ask for your ongoing prayer for the incarcerated cathedral provost Bernhard Lichtenberg, Carthusian monk.

On January 17, 1943, he writes to Sister Stephana, his associate at St. Hedwig's Cathdral:

Nothing else I wish for

but what my Savior wills;
it is why this captive here
ever will hold still.
What the Savior wants is sure,
been made known to men:
Revelation tells of it:
Chapter Two, Verse Ten (Rev. 2:10).

[Revelation 2:10-11, 17 reads:] "Do not fear what you are about to suffer. Beware, the devil is about to throw some of you into prison so that you may be tested, and for ten days you will have affliction. Be faithful until death, and I will give you the crown of life. Let anyone who has an ear listen to what the Spirit is saying to the churches. Whoever conquers will not be harmed by the second death. . . . To everyone who conquers I will give some of the hidden manna, and I will give a white stone, and on the white stone is written a new name that no one knows except the one who receives it."

Suffering from heart disease and a kidney infection, Lich-tenberg writes from his hospital cell at Tegel on September 27, 1943, to Sister Stephana what would be his last letter. A month later, he is discharged from Tegel prison. But the Nazis renege on sending Lichtenberg to the camp at Litzmannstadt. Since they consider him "a danger to the public," he is deported to the concentration camp at Dachau, instead. During a stop-over at Hof, Lichtenberg dies at the local hospital on November 5, 1943.

Praised be Jesus Christ forever and ever. Amen.
Honorable Mother Superior!
For the third time, the good Lord has sent me to the prison hospital. This means I have to write in bed what is likely my

last letter from prison. In looking back over the last two years, I want to and have to give thanks to God from the bottom of my heart, also to all who helped God carry out his holy will for me. I am determined to carry out with God's help the resolutions of the exercises which I made before him when doing the thirty-day [Ignatian] Exercises, namely: I want to see everything that happens to me, joys and sorrows, good news and bad, from the perspective of eternity; I want to be in possession of my soul when it comes to patience, not to sin in word and deed, and to do everything out of love and suffer everything for love's sake.—I have the will to live for another twenty years, but if the good Lord wishes that I die today, then may his holy will be done.

A thousand greetings to the most reverend bishop, to the cathedral chapter, to the parish offices, to the rectory, to the parishioners of St. Hedwig's, to all who have prayed for me and who have written me and thus have given me comfort.

May there ever come to pass, be praised, and eternally honored the most sweet, holy, and righteous will of God, unfathomable in its heights and depths, now and forevermore. Amen.

The prisoner in the Lord
Bernhard Lichtenberg
Provost of the Cathedral of St. Hedwig
—*Bernhard Lichtenberg*, pp. 61-62.

SOURCES

Erb, Alfons. 1947. *Bernhard Lichtenberg: Dompropst von St. Hedwig zu Berlin*. Berlin: Morus.

Feldmann, Christian. 1996. *Wer glaubt, muss widerstehen: Bernhard Lichtenberg—Karl Leisner*. Freiburg: Herder.

Kock, Erich. 1996. *Er widerstand: Bernhard Lichtenberg*. Berlin: Morus.

RUPERT MAYER, S.J.
(1876-1945)

*Munich's "Apostle"
and Evangelist*

Known as the "apostle of Munich," his grave draws up to 3,000 people a day to the crypt of the Bürgersaal Church in downtown Munich. Nearly one-third of a million signatures had petitioned for his beatification, granted in 1987 by Pope John Paul II. Hardly another contemporary figure in German Catholicism commands such wide admiration. War veterans and conscientious objectors, members of traditionalist Catholic men's groups and participants of Catholic youth days and rallies all see in this Jesuit priest—the first German Jesuit to be beatified—someone to look up to. A decorated war veteran and amputee, he had been known for his tireless pastoral and charitable work among the city's poorest and his courage to speak the truth in a kindly straight forward and stubbornly unrelenting way. "They can gun me down," he once said, "but the truth must be told." The truth he proclaimed from Munich's pulpits and chancels, on mission tours in Bavaria, and at public gatherings objected to the regime's forceful secularizing of Catholic schools and the Nazis' slur campaign against Catholic clergy and the church. Restricted first and

149

eventually forbidden to preach altogether, he was pressured into breaking the confessional's secrecy and refused; arrested repeatedly, he was deported to a concentration camp and put in solitary confinement, released again, and finally banned to years in isolation at a Benedictine monastery from where, at war's end, he returned to Munich and where he died the same year while delivering a sermon.

Blessed Rupert Mayer was born the second of six children on January 23, 1876, in Stuttgart. The family was Catholic and economically comfortable. The father came from a long line of merchants, and the parents owned a dry goods store in the predominantly Protestant city. After graduating from the gymnasium, Mayer studied Catholic theology in Fribourg (Switzerland), Munich, and Tübingen. At age twenty-three, he was ordained a priest and one year later entered the Jesuit order. Since Jesuit organizations had been suppressed as part of Germany's culture war under Bismarck, Mayer went first to Feldkirch, Austria, and then to Valkenburg, the Netherlands, where he did his philosophical and theological studies. After serving as assistant to the novice master and completing a practical year, Mayer worked between 1906 and 1911 as a preacher, retreat master of the Ignatian Exercises, and evangelist ("Volksmissionar") in Holland, Germany, Austria, and Switzerland. In 1912, he was sent to Munich by his order's provincial. The cardinal had requested that a Jesuit be assigned to minister to the thousands of Catholics who were flocking from rural villages to the city in search of work. Mayer served as a missionary and chaplain to these uprooted, often unemployed and hence impoverished Catholics and their families. Since attitudes toward church and God could be negative, Mayer reached out through personal home visits, charitable efforts, and newly created pastoral care teams. In 1914, he helped found the Sisters of the Holy Family and became their lifelong spiritual director.

With the outbreak of World War I in 1914, Mayer volunteered with the armed forces. At his insistence, he was moved to the frontlines in January 1915, working as a chaplain of his division in the regions of the Alsace, Galatia, and Rumania. For his courage at the front, his (Protestant) army commander nominated him in August for the Iron Cross First Class, an honor never before given to a Roman Catholic, let alone a professed member of a religious order. Mayer received the cross in December, four weeks prior to losing his left leg during a bomb attack where he had tried to shield with his body a wounded soldier. In 1917, with a newly fitted prosthesis, Mayer returned to Munich and resumed his chaplaincy work. The same year, the Jesuits were allowed again to run their houses, schools, and churches. In 1921, Mayer was appointed pastor, or "Präses," of the Marian congregation of men with its Bürgersaal Church and became a minister at Munich's main Jesuit church, St. Michael's, only steps away from the Bürgersaal. In 1926, he organized a citywide evangelization and mission outreach. The year earlier, he had started a ministry at Munich's central rail station with the argument that if people did not come to church, one had to bring the church to them: On Sundays, Mayer would hold as many as five worship services for weekend travelers and railroad and postal employees, with the first one starting at 3:20 a.m., the last one at 6:35 a.m., then returning from there to St. Michael's downtown to celebrate mass again—several times. While preaching up to seventy times a month, he would spend long hours in the confessional—despite the pain in his leg, raise money for charitable ministries, and help people find jobs.

Mayer regularly studied political propaganda material and frequented political gatherings. When in 1923 he climbed the podium during one of Hitler's political rallies at a Munich beer hall, he was greeted with rousing applause. The gathered crowd assumed they had won over this decorated war hero and one of the city's most popular preachers. But bedlam ensued when he soberly declared, "You have applauded too soon because I will now tell you point blank that a German Catholic can never be National Socialist." Besides, "it's totally incorrect to say that the Gospel is only there for Germanic people." Nonetheless, the next year Mayer received on his silver anniversary as a priest a congratulatory letter from Adolf Hitler.

In 1934, a complaint against Mayer was filed. Nazi spies began taking down Mayer's sermons and monitoring who came to see him. The regime issued a warning to him in 1936 and in the spring of 1937 barred him from preaching outside Munich. His first arrest came in June 1937, followed by a sentence of six months in prison for "abuse of the chancel privilege" and "defamation" against the state. Among the many protesters of Mayer's arrest were Munich's Michael Cardinal von Faulhaber, who had drafted for Pope Pius XI the anti-Nazi encyclical "With Burning Anxiety" (March 1937), and Eugenio Cardinal Pacelli, later to become Pope Pius XII. Upon his release, Mayer declared from the chancel that one had to obey God more than people, which prompted his second arrest in January 1938. Following his release in May, he was prohibited from preaching. His third arrest came in November 1939 for suspicion of being involved in the resistance group "Monarchical Movement." Shortly before Christmas, Mayer was taken to the concentration camp Sachsenhausen-Oranienburg and kept in solitary confinement.

Seven months of concentration camp led to Mayer's rapid decline in health. Fearful of being held responsible by irate crowds for the death of their beloved priest, the Nazi secret police negotiated a way to keep him alive while ensuring his silence. In August 1940, Mayer was transferred to the Benedictine monastery at Ettal in upper Bavaria, where he was placed under permanent house arrest. His mail would be censored. The hearing of confession was disallowed. And contact with the *outside world was prohibited, except for visits by immediate family and doctors. To the preacher with a burning love for souls and people, this was severe punishment indeed. "Since then I am like a living corpse," he said, "for this type of death is to someone like me, still so full of life, much worse than the physical death for which I had often been prepared."*

Shortly after the Americans liberated Ettal on May 11, 1945, Mayer returned to Munich. "If God so chooses," he remarked, "a one-legged Jesuit can outlive a godless dictatorship of a thousand years." Toward the end of May, he delivered a sermon in Munich calling for forgiveness and unity. He eagerly resumed his pastoral duties. Two mild strokes followed in July and September. In early October he relinquished his office as pastor of the Marian congregation, and three weeks later he was dead. Mayer had been preaching at the Cross chapel of St. Michael's when a stroke stopped his speech; for minutes, he remained standing, propped up by his prosthesis, until his confreres carried him out of the church. Within hours, Mayer died at the hospital and soon it was said of him that "Father Mayer never buckled under, not even while dying." He was buried at the Jesuit cemetery in Pullach, south of Munich. When the grave became a pilgrims' site within a short time, it suggested the transfer of his body to Munich. With St. Michael's Church still in ruins, Mayer's remains were taken to the Bürgersaal Church. Three years after his death, on May 23, 1948, more than 30,000 men accompanied the procession that brought Father Mayer's casket from Pullach to Munich.

* * *

For the fortieth anniversary of his ordination to the priesthood, Rupert Mayer celebrated mass at the Sisters of the Holy Family on May 1, 1939. During the festivities, probably after the meal, he gave a summary of his life.

We grew up in a thoroughly Protestant city. Hence our home was like an oasis. We were surrounded by all these anti-Catholic influences. We had to attend a Protestant gymnasium and were given a good many stabs in the ribs so that the good Lord saw to it that my physical strength grew too. Repeatedly I had been chosen captain when it came to competing with another class of students, and that was my good fortune. Once during physical education someone threw himself down before me and said, "That's how you all pray to Mary, isn't it?" I really beat him up good. That was the first and last time. Nobody dared say anything after that. All in all, the [Catholic] influence was very strong and we owe it solely to our parents and especially the father, who from our childhood on drummed into us the Catholic teachings. He used every possible occasion to raise our Catholic self-confidence. And I can say from personal experience that this is formative for a person, and that is comforting to know under the present circumstances. . . .

In religious practice the parents were here formative as well. It became second nature to us that on Sundays and feast days we attended mass. On Sundays, the father always went horseback riding, but he saw to it that one went riding only after he had been to mass. Everyone followed his lead. He had the horse brought to the church and from there one took off. The same is true for the reception of the sacraments. By their practice, the parents showed us that they were serious about religion. . . .

I had a good-size circle of friends and the good Lord saw to it that I became familiar with people's various character traits. This was of great benefit for my future. I was a theologian, but one would have never known that by just looking at me. Hence I had lively contact with people and I began to realize how one can influence people and how incredibly important it is to have a good connection with young people. . . .

Already as a [theology] student I wanted to be in the order. First I flirted with the Dominicans, whom I had met in Fribourg, Switzerland, and then I came in contact with the Jesuits. But then I was prompted by my parents to put the matter on hold. My father said that it was his sincere desire that I should become a diocesan priest. Once I had a position as a diocesan priest, I could do whatever I wanted, and I am grateful to my father that he was firm like that. I became a diocesan priest. . . . Then I the diocesan priest came to a village in the country. I, the diaspora person, was now in a little town that was completely Catholic. It was perfect for my work. What fun, running from here to there, from one sick person to the next and then again back up the mountain. I also was chaplain of the union of apprentices, and though giving speeches was very hard for me at times, I eventually became quite comfortable with it. Still, I always had the feeling that I was lacking the ascetical practice necessary for being a priest. So I always drove to [the Benedictine abbey] Beuron. There I came in contact with the Benedictines. Of course they thought that I would become a Benedictine monk. But while there, my heart always grew so heavy during the beautiful chant. I said to myself: No, I don't fit here; I could not stand it. And I applied with the Jesuits. The bishop said at first, Are you out of your mind, no way, you have to stay with us. And when he came to us for confirmation, he asked me: Do you still want to? Yes, I still do. Okay then, go and make us proud. Then I went to Feldkirch and became a Jesuit priest. The good Lord arranged it all in a remarkable way.

I can only say this about my later life as a priest—struggle and conflicts. I was first a missionary, had to give the Spiritual Exercises and I was always the big fish in the small pond. So it came as a relief to get the order: this one we will send to Munich.

Let's see how things will continue. I always have the feeling that the good Lord will call me home some day quite suddenly, which would fit with my nature. I cannot imagine growing old quietly. Regardless, I only ask that you maintain the direction we have been taking together. We know what kind of work awaits us; how it will all unfold nobody knows and it is not essential to know. The main thing is that we are working for the kingdom of God.   —*Leben im Widerspruch*, pp. 51-55.

Six months after Mayer had spoken at a Hitler rally in a Munich brew house where had had disappointed the audience with his critical remarks about National Socialism, an informant told him in January 1924 that he would be murdered shortly. On April 1, 1924, Mayer wrote a farewell letter to his parents and siblings.

The decision had been made to get rid of me on account of my speeches at the People's Brew House and in Pfaffenhofen and because of my sermons at the Marian congregation in which I felt obligated to point out that the cultural endeavors of the National Socialists were absolutely irreconcilable with the teachings of Christianity and the Catholic Church, and also because I was seen as corrupting the patriotic conscience with my vast influence on the masses. They see me as a detriment to our country, me who during the war saved the lives of dozens of comrades under the greatest peril to his own life. This goes to show as nothing else does that a large segment of our population is in a state of fatal mental confusion, erroneous thinking, and sickness. That is why I gladly forgive my murderers. May the Almighty have mercy on them! I am even grateful to them for wanting to kill me for my apostolic work because it gives me hope to find in God a gracious and merciful judge. I have other reasons that will help me die. But I will take them like a bittersweet secret into my grave and into eternity. Suffice it to say: my life surely was not easy!

May all of this be of comfort to you, dear parents and siblings, as well as to the many dear friends from all circles of society. Even though I have reminded myself daily of how fickle people's affection is and how devious and unreliable many people are, I am still certain that during my life I have met not a few people who truly meant well with me. I want to say a big thank you to the parents, siblings, and all the dear friends for all their love and loyalty they have shown me. On purpose I am not mentioning any names to avoid hurt feelings. Those who were particularly close to me and who have helped me a great deal in doing my work already know who they are and I am shaking their hand as a farewell greeting and giving it a metaphorical squeeze. But those also who have caused me great pain by their insincerity, tactlessness, and envy should know that I am not harboring any ill will against them. May God have mercy on me and on all of them!

I certainly would have liked to continue serving my Lord and my church, the people in need and my poor, defenseless, violated, and disgraced country, but what God does is done well!
— *Leben im Widerspruch*, pp. 164-65.

In 1926, Mayer had overseen the organization of two evangelistic missions in Munich with its three quarters of a million people. At a mission conference in July, he summed up the experience while suggesting concrete steps to take for city pastors in continuing to reach people for Christ.

In preparation [for the mission], it would be of the greatest importance to motivate priests to systematically visit every family [in their parish]. We will later talk about people who are trusted key links, we will later hear about the lay apostolate, the lay assistant; but I insist: there is absolutely no substitute whatsoever for the home visit by the clergy when preparing for a city-wide mission. . . . The work of the parish nun, the work of the [monastic] lay brother is certainly very important; but I always have the terrible worry and concern that their work allows the clergy, ordained for this task of visitation, to move farther and farther away from their own, most integral calling, saying: "The others are doing as good as job as I, so now I can dedicate my precious time to other areas of pastoral care." But it is critical that the pastor, good shepherd that he is, go after the straying little sheep and into their home. Today more so than ever. Why? The situation in the big city is like this: In many cases there is no longer a personal connection with the clergy. I don't mean good Catholics, loyal to their church. We are talking now first and foremost about the unchurched, about this group that sadly makes up seventy percent of the city population and that we are no longer reaching pastorally. I have heard it repeatedly in communist and socialist gatherings: "The priest is a laborer just like we are; he may be better paid [than we are] but is, nonetheless, only a cog in the wheel of capitalism. He gets paid like we do, he dislikes his work just a much as we do; he believes not a word of what he says!" We might deplore this attitude, but it is what it is. That's the atmosphere today in the big city. . . . I don't know a better way of putting a spoke in the wheel of this attitude than the self-sacrificial walk of the clergy to the poor, misled people: Misereor super turbam! When the priest goes up the stairs, down the stairs, when he climbs all the way to the fifth and sixth floors, when he shows his human side, then even the communist has to finally concede: "This man gets nothing, does not get paid [to do this], at the most gets as a wage to be thrown out and insulted." . . . And if the priest shows understanding during these visits, when he is not deterred, even when he gets to hear a great deal of scolding, then perhaps the ice starts to melt. Via the detour of showing understanding for the often sad situation of our people in the city, such as the high rent for a lousy apartment that swallows up one fourth of the salary, a skilled priest will then gradually steer the conversation toward the mission and close with an urgent invitation to it. People in the big city have to feel that even the priest, and he especially, can identify with them. Once again: I know of no other way to reach people in the city than through the home visit, the repeated home visit by the clergy.

—*Leben im Widerspruch*, pp. 174-76.

After 1935, the Jesuits in Germany were subject to special surveillance by the Nazi regime. After 1937, if not before, Mayer had been targeted for surveillance; reports and complete transcripts of ten of his sermons, given mostly in Munich, were found in the archives of the secret police. The following excerpt is from a sermon given on May 2, 1937, after mass at St. Michael's Church, Munich. The introduction by the Nazi informant reads as follows: "The sermon was well attended; in the church were about 1,100 men and women. The mood was of a rather revolutionary type only in the front rows. It appeared that in the very front rows and in the choir loft near the main altar one had positioned claques, whose task it was to clap at the most evocative parts of the sermon! No printed material was distributed!" The Nazi informant's comments are rendered here in brackets and italic type.

Dear Friends! If we do not continue in our [liturgical] cycle today, it has to do with the fact that the current publicity of the sexual misconduct trials [of Catholic clergy] is of such a nature that we need to address it and because I feel obligated to clarify for you the present situation.

In recent times we are reading a lot about the sexual crimes of Catholic priests and members of religious orders. If all of this were true—well, dear friends—then we would have to say that steps need to be taken! It fills us with great concern that these crimes are happening especially now and among the Lord's chosen. But my dear ones, not everything is true that's printed in the paper. The portrayals are exaggerated and sensationalized, and what is printed in the so-called Christian and anti-Catholic newspapers [*with clear and unmistakable reference to the* [Nazi newspaper] *the People's Observer*] is played up big and gutted! The indictment is printed right on the front page in big headlines, then in the following issue there is right on the front page the trial; what the witnesses of the defense are saying is not reported to us at all, and then the incident is exploited in the next issue as a feature story, again on the front page! The other day I read about a priest in the paper who was being tried, a big headline in the paper, but what the charges were, whether he was found guilty or not I have yet to read and I am eagerly waiting for it.

Then we read everywhere about a thousand moral crimes of priests and members of religious orders! This number is vastly exaggerated and as far as I know, there are at the most five hundred cases of which I have read, and perhaps it's only two hundred fifty! But if it truly were a thousand, given that we have in Germany about one hundred thousand religious and priests, then this would be only one percent. It is bad enough that it is happening among us, but it is only one percent! Why is one hearing this only in regard to Catholic and Protestant circles but about the others one never hears anything! Those sitting in a china shop should not be throwing stones. [*Loud murmurs of approval in the front rows, so that Mayer proceeded to calm down the hotheads in the first rows with the remark that these gestures could be easily misinterpreted.*]

What we also object to is the broad and generalizing way of such a portrayal! (*Mayer named a few articles in the People's Observer that did indeed generalize things.*) I read in the People's Observer recently an article about the moral crimes and it said at the end: Every German mother and every German father will think twice now in light of these incidences whether to send their child to such rotten brothers! And it says further in the People's Observer: The monasteries have become the breeding ground for vice and lewdness. It doesn't say "monasteries" but "the monasteries," which is to say that all monasteries are breeding grounds for crime! [*Mayer then proceeded to talk about monastic institutes of higher learning and schools. These schools have proven valuable for decades and why then did the best families send their children to such a school? Why did they entrust their children to these religious orders? A large group of members of religious orders were being attacked here; should they put up with such generalizations?*] We will definitely need to defend ourselves here! We are not revolutionaries, but if things continue like this, we Catholic and Protestant clergy will have to throw a stink bomb in there! We are not putting up with it; we will now fight against it without restraint. [*A scene of Christ on the Mount of Olives. The people are now being asked to do penance for the sordid deeds of the pastors!*]

—*Leben im Widerspruch*, pp. 205-07.

From a sermon of May 23, 1937, preached at 8 p.m. at St. Michael's Church on the occasion of the procession of lights by the Marian Congregation, where about 2,000 men were present from various parishes in Munich. As part of the sermon, Mayer summarizes again newspaper articles denouncing the clergy.

Dear friends! I am completely aware of the responsibility I have taken on with reading this to you. After due consideration, I take on this responsibility in the interest of a person's immortal soul. I am guided by no other thought than the fact that some people are seriously shaken in their faith on account of these terrible newspaper reports. And in order to tell the widest audience possible what the press is doing with such things, how one does not want to serve the truth but wants to fuel hatred against the church, I believe I am obligated to say these things.

Dear friends. To put it in general terms, when one has the impression these days that, well now, you as a priest soon won't be able to show your face in public, then this is something horrible. Don't these people realize that they are robbing 110,000 to 115,000 German men and women of their honor? . . . Those who are turning away from the servants of the church have broken with faith in the church! That's why I have read these things today. They will be useful to you and you should feel free to say that I announced this publicly. . . .

And dear friends, have faith and do not fear! The German episcopacy is united in questions of faith. And not one of the twenty-three bishops is thinking of taking a different route. The leaders of the church in Germany form a united front. They are united with the Holy Father in Rome, one heart and one soul. Remember what this means in our time? The clergy stands behind their bishop, which is the same everywhere. There are always exceptions, those who are confused. It still means that behind the clergy stands the entire Catholic people. And when one realizes how Catholics are slowly waking up, how they begin to understand what is happening, then one is deeply heartened by it.

Therefore, do not fear! Have faith! Trust in Jesus Christ! He is the joy of our life, the power of our life, the comfort of our life. He is our friend, our Alpha and Omega, beginning and end. Trust in him! How easy he has made it for all those who are dying! How often I have witnessed and seen this with my own eyes! Then one realizes the power of our sacred faith. Trust in him! How beautifully he often says: "Take courage, I have conquered the world"; for whoever conquers the world has the victory. In the first place, trust in Jesus Christ.

Therefore, dear friends, we are striving eagerly and earnestly

to get ever closer to our Savior. This happens through culti-
vating a (. . . ?) life. The times are serious. And that we owe
to the enemies of the church, since they have forced us into
self-reflection so that once more many people are taking more
seriously their religious obligations. Sermons have never seen
such a high attendance, and the same goes for worship services
and the reception of the sacraments. How precious this is! Not
the outward battles are leading to victory! No! Our relationship
with Jesus Christ becomes the foundation of a new awakening
in religious matters. And those who are fortified on the inside
will invariably show it on the outside and will have nothing to
be afraid of. If only he is with us. And if the whole world were
filled with devils, we will not fear. Save for him they cannot
harm us. For this reason I want to commend to you monthly
communion. And do not forget the holy exercises. Those who
have gone through this school [of the exercises] will be fortified,
we can count on it. If, God forbid, push came to shove, it will
become clear that the Catholic faith is anchored much more
deeply in the hearts of millions than it might have looked at
times. Therefore, let us meet the future with glad courage. If
Christ is for us, who can be against us? Nobody! Then we are
safe and secure now and forever. Amen!

—*Leben im Widerspruch*, pp. 211-14.

*In April and May, preaching injunctions were issued against
Mayer with which he did not comply and in which he was
supported by his provincial, Augustin Rösch, S.J. On June 5,
1937, he was arrested the first time. Asked by Nazi officials to
restrain himself in his sermons so as to be left in peace, Mayer
made the following statement.*

I declare that in case of my release I will, based on fundamental convictions, continue to preach both in the churches
in Munich and in the rest of Bavaria despite the preaching

injunction. I especially declare that also in the future I will defend the church from the pulpit against any attacks with all decisiveness and honesty and sharpness the same as before, but without any personal attack. I will continue to preach in the way I have been, even if the government, the police, and the courts should consider my sermons given from the pulpit as acts to be punishable by law and abuse of the pulpit privilege.

—*Leben im Widerspruch*, p. 218.

Mayer was released on July 23, 1937, arrested again on January 5, 1938, and released on May 3, 1938. His third arrest was on November 3, 1939, resulting in his deportation on December 24, 1939, to the concentration camp Sachsenhausen-Oranienburg; from there he was transferred on August 7, 1940, to the Ettal monastery, where he was put under permanent house arrest. From all these prisons Mayer tried to send letters, but his requests were often denied or the letters never reached the addressee.

A letter to the inspector of the Nazi secret police, Otto Gambs, was written on June 22, 1937, but intercepted and filed with the trial documents, where it remains to this day.

Dear Mr. Inspector,

In reference to the conversation we once had in your office, I am enclosing this news clipping [about the number of priests and religious involved in moral crime trials]. You see that in this matter you were poorly informed. I would kindly ask you to forward this clipping to the lady who sat at the typewriter. When you did visit me once in my humble place at St. Michael's, you smiled when I told you that I would end up in prison—and now? And when I once predicted that I would die in prison, you would not believe me. At least that is what you indicated—and yet that is precisely what will happen—unless

I should outlive this present regime, something you certainly don't think will happen. But I am in no way unhappy about it. Actually, I feel quite well and contented. I am completely at peace with my situation. If only people understood how little it takes to be truly happy. I have always known that God is good, but that he is this good, as I have come to find out during these last fourteen days, I would never have thought possible.

By the way, I and all the other priests who are in prison for similar reasons as mine will eventually lie heavily in the state's stomach! Unfortunately! To my great sorrow. But the state is asking for it. If I ever were to come free again, since nothing is impossible with God, I will give our last chauffeur a lesson about the need to be civil with every single member of the Volk, even if this member is a "black one" [a priest].

> With best wishes,
> Rupert Mayer, S.J.

Margin notation: Please don't work too hard; no one will thank you for it, unless you are doing your work out of love for God. Enclosures: Text from "Kettelerfeuer," No. 24, 1937 [a Catholic weekly]. Title of the text: "The Ratio of the Number of Trials of Priests and Religious and the Total Number of Catholic Priests and Religious."

—*Leben im Widerspruch*, p. 371.

Letter from the Landsberg prison to his provincial, Augustin Rösch, S.J. in Munich, dated January 30, 1938; the letter never reached the provincial but was retained for "abuse of the letter-writing privilege."

Most Reverend, dear Father!
Finally I am able to write you a few lines. I would rather tell

you a few things than my family members. Please share with my mother what you deem appropriate.

One thing seems of special importance: What I have done I would do all over again, step by step. And now I am much rather in prison than outside with its obligation to comply with the preaching injunction. Since then the pressure on my conscience has eased up. Therefore, please do not allow [Dr. Joseph] Warmuth to file an appeal for a shortening of the sentence. I would much rather stay in prison for as long as possible than again being taken into police custody [at the Wittelsbacher Palais in Munich]; since I refuse to keep the preaching injunction, I will invariably end up getting arrested again. Even though life at the Wittelsbacher Palais is more comfortable [than at Landsberg], there was nothing there for religious edification and these barbarians let people die "without lux or crux" [sacraments for the dying]. While I may be receiving communion here only once a month, at least one is surrounded by religious air. The worship services are quite beautiful. People like to go; in many of them there still is so much good will. Perhaps you noticed my irritation with the staff during our last meeting at the Wittelsbacher Palais; I had good reasons for it. Perhaps I will have the opportunity sometime to tell you about them. By the way, I am completely done with life; I would not object to it if I were never to be released from prison. I now consider my life's task completed. Therefore, no appeal! . . .

I have the opportunity here to practice extreme poverty. Toothbrush, comb and soap, rosary, breviary and (. . .) were the only things I was able to rescue: yes, also the boots because I cannot walk in any others. It is hard to believe how little a person really needs. That goes for the food too. Only because I promised it to you do I force myself to eat. I would be a natural when it comes to dying of starvation. It would not be hard for me. What is hard is eating, especially when I consider that I have to clean it all up afterwards with greasy rags or at least dry it . . .

My whole life I never had to do manual labor, not even in my youth; all my free time was spent with music, gymnastics, sword and sable fencing, swimming, horseback riding and driving. And now these unpractical two hands! . . .

—*Leben im Widerspruch*, pp. 381-82.

Since the first letter was denied, Mayer writes a second letter to his provincial the next day, January 31, 1938; it was intercepted also.

I ask you, Most Reverend Father, to continue as before and not to make any concessions about the prohibition to preach. I know well what will befall me when I get out of here; but I prefer to live in prison rather than giving even the slightest impression that one were intending to obey the state's preaching injunction. . . .

I am now as poor as a church mouse. That is great. It serves me very well. I am so glad to be left in peace! With the way I feel I could easily sail off into this other, better world of the beyond. My death would be hurting a few people, but it would only be temporary. It is bound to happen one day. Whether it happens five or ten years earlier is completely irrelevant.

I hope that the work of the Jesuit priests at St. Michael's and elsewhere can proceed without obstacles. I am thinking a lot of my fellow sufferer in Nuremberg [Alois Jung, S.J., also in prison]. Many greetings to him and to all the known Jesuits and brothers in the various houses! . . .

Do not forget Warmuth!

No letters, gifts, visits are going through! Everything is in vain! Only prayer and doing penance helps! That is our weapon

by which we will gain victory for the kingdom of God.
                                —*Leben im Widerspruch*, pp. 385-86.

Mayer was interned at the concentration camp Sachsenhau-sen-Oranienburg between December 24, 1939, and August 7, 1940, where the Protestant pastor Martin Niemöller was be-ing held also. From there Mayer was moved to Ettal and put under house arrest. His provincial, Augustin Rösch, had Mayer record his remembrances about the camp. Probably in 1943, Mayer dictated his impressions to a Benedictine monk at Et-tal, Richard Bauersfeld, O.S.B., who then typed them up. The manuscript, titled "National Socialism and I" ("Der National-Sozialismus and meine Wenigkeit"), is Mayer's longest text, and it is excerpted here. Mayer produced a shorter version on October 13, 1945, for the Military Tribunal that became part of the Nuremberg Documents (PS 3272).

By the previously said I already indicted that I cannot com-plain about the treatment. After all, I was in the prison of a concentration camp. One had to make peace with that. What was beneficial to me there was that I could devote my entire time to prayer and studies. Right from the start I was told that I would not be enlisted for physical labor, could freely dispose of my time. And that was upheld. Naturally the meals were meager.

As I heard later, there was much talk among the public about Pastor Niemöller in connection with me, so that it was said, among other things: through my influence, Pastor Niemöller became Catholic, etc. I have to stress that all this talk was nothing but fantasies. True is that at the concentration camp I never saw Pastor Niemöller. Sure, I had been told that he was in the concentration camp Sachsenhausen, but that is all I knew.

However, I did have the burning desire to see Pastor

Niemöller at least once and talk to him. Since this was not possible, at least daily I remembered him, his heavily tested family, and his heavy cross. I hoped that by doing so I would be able to afford some reprieve for him, who for such a long time lived so close to me.

—*Leben im Widerspruch*, p. 128.

During his five years at Ettal, Mayer was allowed to see family members and his doctor. He also had several conversations with Dietrich Bonhoeffer, who spent three months at Ettal, between November 1940 and February 1941. But he was not permitted to hear confession, officiate at mass or preach if outsiders were present, and provide pastoral care to visitors and the public.

Based on my fundamental attitude toward the church's office, I had no choice but to give in. When the prelate said that the church administration thought that this would only be temporary, that in the course of time the restrictions would be eased, I could only shake my head with incredulity. As it turns out, I was right.

Since then I am like a living corpse, for this type of death is to someone like me, still so full of life, much worse than the physical death for which I had often been prepared. To the secret police and the entire Nazi movement I could and can do no bigger favor than to quietly wither away here, for now the secret police has saved face before the Catholic people, some of whom have not yet forgotten me. The dear people are saying to themselves: He actually has it quite good since he went to the monastery. Who knows what might have happened to him if he had stayed in Munich. These dear people do not understand what the life that I am forced to lead here really means for me, as I have indicated above. They also do not know that the air raids are much more heart-breaking to me here than if I were right in the middle of them in Munich. I have not run away—though I would not mind being arrested for it or having my head cut off—because there are several considerations that compel me to stay:

1. Consideration for the monastery, which is responsible for me and whom I would cause great problems if I were to violate the conditions of the secret police. But this I am not inclined to do since from the start of my stay here I have been treated with the greatest respect, even with great love, beginning with the most reverend abbot all the way to the lowest-ranking employee of the monastery I have had dealings with. No difficulties have been caused me by them; on the contrary, as far as one could ease conditions for me in light of the harsh stipulations by the secret police, one has done so. That should always be acknowledged with the deepest gratitude. Thus, it was made possible for me from the time of my arrival in August 1942 through November to swim daily in the splendidly situated pond, since the pond is on the property of the monastery, etc.

2. Consideration of my order, whom I would have certainly caused considerable problems with an escape from Ettal.

3. Consideration for some dear, good people, who would suffer great sorrow by my repeated incarceration or the potential deportation to a concentration camp or my death as a result.

4. Consideration for the good Lord, to whom I have decidedly drawn closer, as probably never before in my life, during the long years of carrying my cross and the resulting gradual detachment from all earthly and temporal things. Should I now force a break by my own willful

doing in this straight line that I have been keeping by the grace of God day in and day out? From the standpoint of the faith I believe that I have to say a hearty no here. Therefore, I want to continue to carry my cross and do penance and suffer for my own mistakes and weaknesses until the good Lord decides to take this cross away. For the time ahead, too, my motto will be: nearer, my God, to thee. And I want to help make it possible through daily conscientious work, through suffering and prayer for all blinded people who did not know what they were doing and who do not know it even to this day, for our terribly afflicted nation, for all souls who have been entrusted to me during my long life as a priest, and especially for all who by their prayer and at times extraordinary sacrifice have helped me bear the heavy cross, that we may one day see one another again and with the vision and in possession of God will be able to rejoice eternally. May God grant it!

—*Leben im Widerspruch*, pp. 134-36.

At the end of the war, Mayer returned to Munich and preached on the main feast of the Marian Congregation of Men in Munich on May 27, 1945. Several thousand men had gathered in St. Ludwig's Church in a city, 90 percent destroyed, where one-third of a million people were homeless and nearly seven thousand had lost their lives during bomb attacks.

Today I am preaching my first sermon after the hard war. The good Lord has granted me freedom again. It took such a long time and I did not believe that I would be able to preach again to you, my dear men. I also did not expect to come here again. For the longest time I had been anticipating only a reunion in eternity.

While at the concentration camp in Oranienburg, I could clearly see that things were bound to go the way I had envisioned. It was during one evening that my heart grew heavy and for two nights I made imaginary visits to you. I visited the churches where I had preached and the families that knew me and I said my farewells, said goodbye as if one would not see one another again in this world. I am not embarrassed to tell you that during these two nights I cried at the thought of having now departed from all these dear, good people. But the good Lord had other plans. It turned out different than what I had thought. I know that this is what the good Lord intended. Contrary to my expectations this has happened and the good Lord has sent me out again and I can only say: I am deeply grateful to God, for he is good and his mercy lasts from one generation to the next for those who love him. All praise and honor and glory be to the most holy and eternal Father, the Son, and the Holy Spirit! Besides God I feel obligated to thank all the good people who have had a share in what has happened on account of their prayers and sacrifice. But first and foremost I am indebted to you, members of the sodality; for I know it from my colleagues that I owe you the deepest gratitude.

Dear friends! Since we saw one another last, something terrible has happened to you too. With deep pain and bitter sorrow I heard about it all, and everything was told to me that you and your loved ones had to endure during all these years. I was already back here in Munich when I heard that so many of your homes had been burned down and bombed. One says it so easily and has heard it so frequently that this one's home has been bombed and was burned down. Some people say it because it is how one generally phrases it. But today I am mindful of what this means for the individual family. I have tried to imagine what it means to the woman and the children, to the family, to immediate family members and relatives. Dear friends! When a person no longer has clothes, linens, a coat, a home, nothing at all of what is necessary for leading a reasonably human life, when the family has been more or less beaten into the ground, then this is something quite terrible. My dear friends! People often have no idea what to do now. The business is completely ruined: How to make a living, how to earn what is needed? And then the thought of our loved ones at the front: What will they say when they come home and find nothing of what had been dear and precious to them? The entire family history is gone, all the pictures and photographs from youth, childhood. Nothing of it exists anymore. What damage to the future of family life. And still, dear friends, and this is a very big comfort, it is not the result of an accident, it has happened like that (. . .). Our Lord has allowed it, has destined it like that! If he has destined it like that, then it was well! He has given and he has taken away! "Whatever God ordains is for the good" [the opening line of a popular hymn]. We certainly cannot yet understand and comprehend the reason. We would have arranged it differently. But if God has ordained it like that, then it was well. . . .

And something else, dearly beloved: In remembering the loved ones who have died, we should not dwell on what we lost. Don't always ponder it, meditate on it. Reading about it each day makes it hard, one should not do that. It is not good to daily recall the hard times. We must not think only of what we have lost with the death of a loved one but also of what our loved one has gained. He would not want to trade with us, he has entered the kingdom of light and glory. He is with God. Through God he has obtained everything. . . .

[In closing] I should like to add one thing that needs to be told the entire foreign press throughout the world. They are saying: "How could the German people stand by and witness the horror of the concentration camps; why did they not protest?" Only a few words of explanation! The German people, meaning the simple folk, the common people could not do anything about it. They simply vanished and their disappearance did nothing to help matters. It is a great injustice and only shows that those who are writing things like that have no grasp of the situation in which we have lived for so long. The simple people cannot be held responsible. On the other hand, I admit that there were highly educated, highly respected and capable people, people of high repute in Germany who could have gained a hearing among the allies and also among the German people if only they had put their head on the chopping block and had drawn attention to this situation. But this, too, required enormous effort. So, dear friends, one cannot blame other people. It will come out sooner or later how many clergy members defended this catastrophic worldview. We know that a good many members of the clergy sat in prison for years and also suffered, so that many capable people gave their lives for the cause.

Now, though, we want to make it clear, dear friends, that the kingdom of God will be presently arising again. But it needs help and helpers. Let us rejoice! No one may say I don't count. God's church needs helpers from every corner of our nation. And we don't want to shirk off our responsibility. As far as it depends on us, we will meet the call to the apostolate from our congregation. With our whole heart we will stand up for Christ's kingdom, for God's church! Amen.

—*Leben im Widerspruch*, pp. 399-407.

Upon his return to Munich, Mayer worked tirelessly and compassionately to assist people in their needs. As part of his pastoral care efforts, he wrote 324 letters to the authorities. The largest share, eighty of these letters, are requests of clemency for those who had belonged to the Nazi party and now suffered from the allies' de-Nazification measures, such as job loss or internment, as well as for former secret police (SS) employees, since the Nuremberg War Court had declared the SS a "criminal organization."

I hereby declare that I have known Ms. E.K. of Munich for quite some time and that I had with her several in-depth conversations and that I am firmly convinced that this woman has credibility. It is also important to know that Ms. K. has repeatedly refused to take her children out of the church and has raised them, despite the severest threats, in the Catholic faith. Her husband belonged to the SS, but Ms. K. herself never had any connection with the SS, on the contrary, she refused to accept from her husband any kind of alimony for the raising of the six children. This is a rare case, which makes me bold to suggest that the seizing of her bank assets be lifted.

—Letter of Recommendation, July 19, 1945;
Leben im Widerspruch, p. 410.

As I have been told, Mr. H. of M. has been relieved of his position as principal teacher. Mr. H. is considered an excellent Catholic teacher throughout the region. He is ever willing to become engaged in Catholic causes and he is a very good influence on the children entrusted to him, which the church community appreciates greatly. For that reason, the people are disturbed that he has been relieved of his office. The reason for his joining the [Nazi] party was because during these crazy times it was considered proper form for teachers to belong to the party; otherwise, this good-natured Catholic teacher would never have joined the party. Personally he never had anything in common with the aims of the Nazi party. I urgently request that the matter of Mr. H.'s dismissal as principal teacher be reconsidered.

—To the Military Regime, Munich, August 16, 1945;
Leben im Widerspruch, p. 411.

The family B. of Munich has been told recently that their apartment was confiscated and they would have to move to the barracks. The situation is like this: Mr. B. was a fanatical member of the Nazi party. He admits that he has erred gravely and is willing to suffer any form of punishment. But what deeply upsets him is that he has dragged his wife and his two children into this misery. For fourteen years the wife had been trying with all imaginable means to dissuade him from his Nazi convictions because she herself and her children were fiercely opposed to National Socialism. This entire time she has had to suffer endlessly and now, to make matters worse, she is being thrown out of her home. She has said, however, that she would now stand by her husband and would defend him because he has had to endure many insults from various sides. In this terrible misfortune that has come upon her, she no longer has any reproach left in her toward her husband because she sees that he is near despair.

Therefore I am requesting that the confiscation of the apartment be lifted as far as wife and children are concerned. The neighbors would see the confiscation of the apartment as an injustice against the woman and the children because the woman's persistent convictions in regard to the Nazi regime are widely known.

—To the Military Regime, Munich, August 29, 1945;
Leben im Widerspruch, pp. 412-13.

Ms. G., née W., has been dismissed from her position in public service. During her employment with the secret police (SS), this woman has provided me and my brothers in the order with extraordinary services. She warned several of my brothers, who undoubtedly would have been arrested without her warning. She did it despite the ever-present danger that if her doings were discovered she would be subject to the severest punishment.

All this time she refused to join the party, hence was already suspect. Regardless, she held out at her post in order to do good, even though she would have much preferred to quit her job with the SS, which, based on personal conversations with her, I know for a fact. I request that the dismissal be kindly reconsidered and that she be reinstated.

—Recommendation for Ms. G, October 1, 1945;
Leben im Widerspruch, pp. 413-14.

SOURCES

Feldmann, Christian. 1987. *Die Wahrheit muß gesagt werden: Rupert Mayer—Leben im Widerstand*. Freiburg: Herder.

Mayer, Rupert. 1991. *Leben im Widerspruch: Autobiographische Texte, Prozeß vor dem Sondergericht, Reden und Briefe*. Ed. Roman Bleistein, S.J. Frankfurt am Main: Josef Knecht Verlag.

—